50
UNUSUAL
THINGS
to see in
ONTARIO

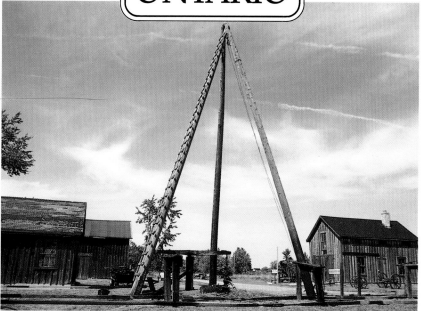

The dune that ate a town.

50
UNUSUAL
THINGS
to see in
ONTARIO

RON BROWN

THE BOSTON MILLS PRESS

CANADIAN CATALOGUING IN PUBLICATION DATA

Brown, Ron, 1945-
Fifty unusual things to see in Ontario

ISBN 0-919783-87-2

1. Ontario - Description and Travel - 1981 -
Guide-books. 2. Curiosities and wonders -
Ontario.   I. Title

FC3057.B76 1989   917.13'044   C89-94072-X
F1057.B76 1989

03 02 01 00 99   4 5 6   7 8

Reprinted in 1999 by
BOSTON MILLS PRESS
132 Main Street
Erin, Ontario N0B 1T0
Tel 519-833-2407
Fax 519-833-2195
e-mail books@boston-mills.on.ca
www.boston-mills.on.ca

An affiliate of
STODDART PUBLISHING CO. LIMITED
34 Lesmill Road
Toronto, Ontario, Canada
M3B 2T6
Tel 416-445-3333
Fax 416-445-5967
e-mail gdsinc@genpub.com

Distributed in Canada by
General Distribution Services Limited
325 Humber College Boulevard
Toronto, Canada M9W 7C3
Orders 1-800-387-0141 Ontario & Quebec
Orders 1-800-387-0172 NW Ontario & Other Provinces
e-mail customer.service@ccmailgw.genpub.com
EDI Canadian Telebook S1150391

Distributed in the United States by
General Distribution Services Inc.
85 River Rock Drive, Suite 202
Buffalo, New York 14207-2170
Toll-free 1-800-805-1083
Toll-free fax 1-800-481-6207
e-mail gdsinc@genpub.com
www.genpub.com
PUBNET 6307949

Typography by Lexigraf, Tottenham
Cover design by Gillian Stead
Printed in Singapore

All photographs in this book are by the author unless otherwise noted.

Contents

Acknowledgements

Introduction

THE NORTHWEST

1. The Castle on White Otter Lake
2. Gold Rock
3. The Thunder Bay Mesas
4. Legend of Silver Islet
5. Ghost Railway to Nowhere
6. Grand Canyon North: Ouimet Canyon

THE NORTHEAST

7. Moosonee: On the Frontier Fringe
8. Cobalt's Boomtown Legacy
9. The Algoma Central:
   A Train Ride from the Past
10. Cockburn Island:
    A Ghost Island Township
11. Taste of the Appenines:
    Sudbury's Little Italy
12. Happy Valley and the Hill of Fire
13. The White Crests of Killarney
14. A Viewpoint with a Difference
15. Stonehenge Ontario?
16. Kapuskasing:
    A Planned Town in the Northern Bush

EASTERN ONTARIO

17. The Ruins of St. Raphael
18. Garden Island
19. Ontario's Smallest Ferry
20. Lake on the Mountain
21. The Other Long Point
22. The Dune That Ate a Town
23. Bell Rock Water-Powered Sawmill
24. Waterway from the Past;
    The Hand-Operated Rideau Canal
25. Going Backwards Up a Hill

COTTAGE COUNTRY

26. The Teaching Rocks:
    Peterboro's Petroglyphs
27. The Last Giants
28. The Opeongo: A Mountain Road
29. The Nipissing Road of Broken Dreams
30. Madill Log Church
31. Boats on Rails:
    The Big Chute Marine Railway
32. There's a Boat Over Your Head:
    The Trent Canal Lift Locks
33. Eight Sides to a House
34. Depot Harbour:
    A Ghost Town Worth Visiting
35. Thirty Thousand Islands

THE SOUTHWEST

36. Cabot Head: Remote Tranquility
37. Petrolia Discovery
38. Return of the Fleet: Port Dover
39. Horse and Buggy Days:
    In Defence of Mennonite Watching
40. The Last Covered Bridge
41. Paris Plains Church
42. Fort Mississauga: The Forgotten Fort
43. The Great Greenock Swamp
44. The Schoolhouse That Rode the Rails

AROUND TORONTO

45. Ontario's Badlands
46. Ghost Canal
47. Temple of Light
48. The Dutch Chapel
49. Toronto Islands' Haunted Lighthouse
50. North Toronto CPR:
    The Station That Wasn't

About the Author

Acknowledgements

I owe much to the many who provided ideas and information for this book. Institutions such as Ontario's ministries of Tourism and Recreation, and Natural Resources, as well as Inco in Sudbury, generously shared their resources. Thanks, too, to the many individuals who shared their time and thoughts. They are too numerous to list completely, but paramount among them are Dick Ellis, Gord Carter, Dave Burcholtz, Matt Rukavina, Lloyd Walton, Sonja Kokal, Margaret Sloman, and James K. Barker, district manager of the Ministry of Natural Resources' Minden office. And special thanks, too, to my family, June, Jeri and Ria, who stoutly suffered my spur-of-the-moment dashes about the countryside in a seemingly endless search for ever more unusual things.

Introduction

Hurtling along Highway 400 or careening madly along the MacDonald Cartier Freeway, have you ever suppressed the urge to exit at random and simply explore? Next time let the urge win out. Follow that road with the interesting name and what you find along it may delight and astonish you.

Ontario's countryside and even its cities are chock full of visual delights. Beaches, mountains and historic streetscapes wait at nearly every turn. Tourist books and travel articles lavish type upon them and ensure that you will not be alone.

Yet among the better-known attractions there are those little-known few — a canal that never saw water, a railway car that routinely hauls an 80-foot yacht from one lake to the next, a mysterious lake on the lip of a mountain, a golden ghost town that has sat silent and virtually untouched for three quarters of a century, a magnificent railway station that saw hardly any passengers. These are just a few of Ontario's unusual things. And they await you, intrepid explorer.

What is an "unusual thing"? For this pernicious prober it is anything that is unexpected. Something that shouldn't belong where you found it. The book you now hold will help you get to 50 of them. Most you can drive to; a few require a bit more effort. But even if you only sit at home and read about them, you will soon understand how many wonderfully unusual things are to be found in our province.

Before you leave home, plan ahead. The maps in this book are only guides. For more detailed routings pick up a copy of the provincial road map issued by the Ministry of Transportation. They are free and they are good. If you are in search of something a little harder to get to, then phone the municipality. Staff in most municipal offices are knowledgeable, helpful and will be delighted to see you. Be sure to check your camera and take extra film. Then, if you like what you find in this book, carry on. Follow the road around the next bend and over the next hill. You may find a hidden lake, a magnificent view, an eerie abandoned mansion, or . . .

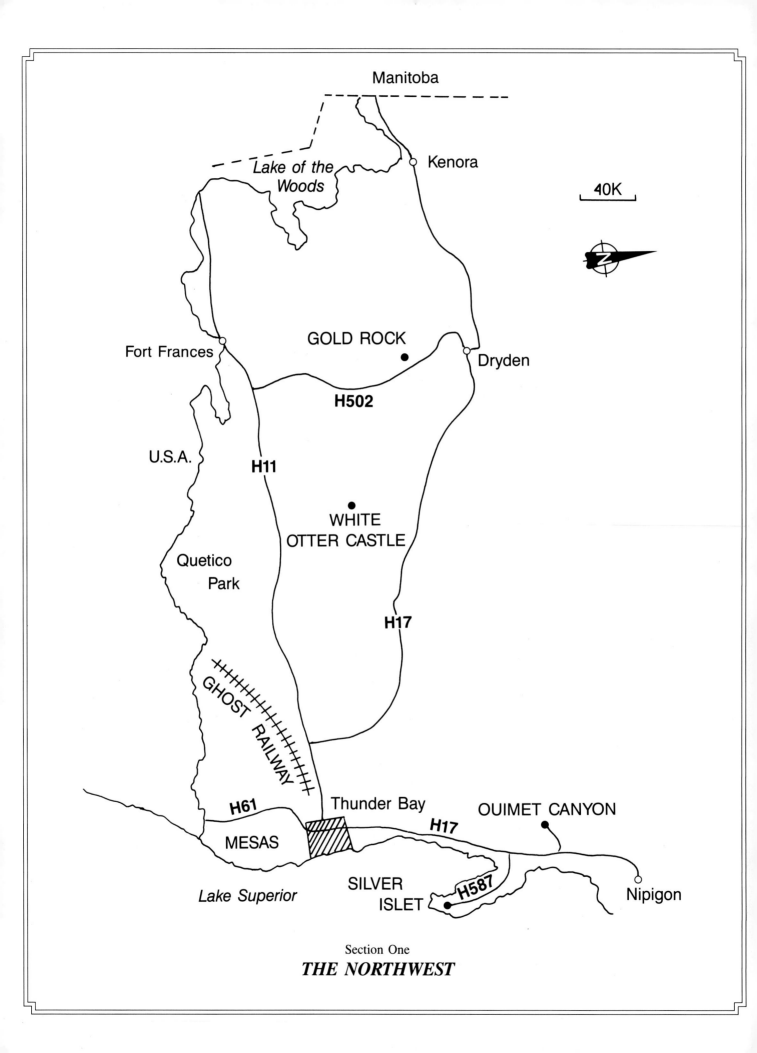

Manitoba

Lake of the
Woods

Kenora

40K

N

GOLD ROCK

Fort Frances

Dryden

H502

U.S.A.

H11

WHITE
OTTER CASTLE

Quetico
Park

H17

GHOST RAILWAY

H61

Thunder Bay

H17

OUIMET CANYON

MESAS

Lake Superior

SILVER
ISLET

H587

Nipigon

Section One
THE NORTHWEST

1
The Castle on White Otter Lake

Those things which are the hardest to reach often offer the richest rewards. This is the case with the strange castle on White Otter Lake near Ignace in far northwestern Ontario.

Four portages and a day's canoeing from the nearest road, this four-storey mansion was constructed entirely of logs by a wiry little man, only 5 feet 7 inches, with no help and no machinery.

In 1887 James A. McOuat arrived in Canada from Scotland to carve out a farm in the wilderness of northwestern Ontario. A decade of inconsistent crops followed. Then came the cry, "Gold!" The northwestern Ontario gold rush was on and McOuat joined the stampede into the bush. But he fared no better at prospecting than he had at farming. Determined to show his worth to society and, it is said, to attract the love of a lady, McOuat decided to build a castle. He chose a sand beach on the northwest arm of White Otter Lake. Here, facing west, he could enjoy his favourite image, the spectacular northwestern sunset.

He carefully chose the best red pine logs, hand winched them through the bush, squared them on three sides and carefully dovetailed the ends to make an airtight fit. By using skids, holes, and pegs, McOuat patiently and painstakingly inched the logs up the walls until finally his tower stood four storeys high. The main living area stood two storeys.

Contrary to later legend, McOuat was neither a hermit nor an eccentric. Rather he enjoyed company and travelled frequently to the busy railway town of Ignace, the nearest supply point. In fact, in the pre-road era such isolated living was common. McOuat was proud of his achievement and often showed off photographs of his home.

The irony was that his castle was never his own, for he had squatted on Crown Land (also common in those days). For three years he carried on a futile effort to acquire title. The Department of Lands and Forests (the predecessor to today's Ministry of Natural Resources), unimpressed by his remarkable feat, repeatedly denied him title to his own home. The dispute abruptly ended when in October 1918 James McOuat became tangled in his fishing nets only metres away from his castle and drowned.

For seven decades his castle has stood empty, a victim of weather but generally free from vandals. Today the Ministry of Natural Resources has decided it doesn't want the castle after all and would rather demolish it. However determined heritage enthusiasts from Atitkokan and Ignace, calling themselves the Friends of White Otter, have rallied to save it. In early 1989 consultants unveiled a $1 million plan to preserve and partially restore the now rickety structure.

You can reach White Otter Castle on your own by canoe from a local logging road in less than a day. Or you can join the Friends of the White Otter on their summer pilgrimages to the site, where you can wonder at the work of one small but determined man. As you watch the sun set over the quiet northern lake, you will understand why Jimmy McOuat called it home.

The log White Otter Castle was built by one man alone in the bush.- Ontario Ministry of Natural Resources

2
Gold Rock

Gold rushes are nothing new to northern Ontario. From the earliest mad dash into the Seine River country west of Thunder Bay in the 1880s to the frenzied activity at Hemlo, far to the north of Sault Ste. Marie, in the 1980s, all conjure an aura of glitter and glamour.

Most of these rushes transformed an area of forest into noisy mines and lusty boom towns. With the exhaustion of the ore, many of these towns declined into sleepy service villages content to reflect upon their memories of former greatness. Others, like Gold Rock near Dryden, were abandoned and have been almost completely reclaimed by the forest.

By 1901 Klondike fever had run its course and prospectors had begun to filter back to the more familiar fields of northwestern Ontario. Here, on the shores of the Manitou lakes, they resumed the searches that had been interrupted by the golden ghosts of the Yukon.

Although it paled beside the world-famous Klondike, the Manitou field did show promise. W.A. Blackstone led the way with the Bigmaster Mine in 1902, and by 1906 half a dozen mines were banging away on the shores of the lake.

Nearby, a supply town appeared and took the name Gold Rock. Its hotels, churches and school all became the focus for the scattered mining camps and linked them with the outside by a wagon road and steamer to Wabigoon on the C.P.R. But by the time World War One took over the headlines, many of the Gold Rock mines had become victims of high-grading, mismanagement or fraud. The town fell silent and the forest took over.

Six decades later, when historical researchers from Ontario's Ministry of Natural Resources reached the shores of the lake, they found an unexpected sight. Many of the mining structures from the turn of the century were still intact. Too remote for vandals, mills, cabins and headframes peaked everywhere from the forest. Although a few buildings in the Gold Rock townsite had been removed to make way for a small fishing camp, Gold Rock, the researchers wrote, contained Ontario's best

A turn-of-the-century gold mill lurks from the forest at Gold Rock.

collection of heritage mining buildings. (However another decade has passed since their report and that ministry still dithers over the future of this remarkable heritage site.)

Roads creep ever closer. Today you can drive south on Highway 502 from Dryden to within six kilometres of the site and follow the remains of the old wagon road the rest of the way. If you're not intimidated by the eerie stillness of the northern bush, you will find this a fairly easy afternoon's adventure. And at the end you will be rewarded with the sights from a gold rush of long ago.

3
The Thunder Bay Mesas

Say the word "mesas" and, as with "ghost towns," the mind immediately travels to western American deserts. Neither the mind nor the body need leave northwestern Ontario, for near the city of Thunder Bay spreads a landscape of mesas that equals most spectacles the West has to offer.

Here on the northwestern shore of Lake Superior the rocks are older than anywhere else on earth. The best guess at their age puts them at 600,000,000 years. Why then have the relentless forces of erosion not ground them into the round rocky knobs found in the Haliburton and Muskoka area, the kind more commonly associated with the Canadian Shield?

Those mysteries lie with an ancient sea that deposited layer upon layer of clay and fine silt which compressed over countless millennia into an unusually hard caprock. As erosion wore away the softer rocks beneath, the caprock resisted and created the landscape of mesas that dominates Thunder Bay's horizon.

They are at their most spectacular right around Thunder Bay itself, where the looming Mt. MacKay provides the highest urban lookout in Ontario. Lining Highway 61, which leads southwest to the U.S. border, the brooding mesas contrast with the lush and prosperous farmland that spreads at their feet.

Thunder Bay's most famous mesa is the Sleeping Giant, the mythical resting place of the legendary Indian named Nanabozo. When viewed from Thunder Bay the mesa resembles a sleeping human form.

In reality the Sleeping Giant is a series of four mesas that form the backbone of the Sibley Peninsula and provide users of Sleeping Giant Provincial Park with some of the most spectacular hiking trails in Ontario.

But the dramatic climax of this awesome landscape lies at the foot of the Sleeping Giant, where Thunder Cape towers 300 metres, or nearly a third of a mile, above the dark, tossing waters of Lake Superior.

Mesa: a high rocky tableland with precipitous sides (The Concise Oxford Dictionary).

Overleaf:
Thunder Bay's Sleeping Giant rock formation is made up of four mesas. Here it is seen from the less familiar east side.

4
The Legend of Silver Islet

Today the beach at the foot of the Sibley Peninsula near Thunder Bay is a place where children play and adults absorb the warm summer sun. But when the wind shifts tot he northwest and brings the first snowflakes of fall, the ghost town of Silver Islet falls silent to reflect upon memories of when it was Canada's greatest silver town.

More than a century ago, mining magnate Alexander Sibley and engineer William Frue set out to tame the wild waters of Lake Superior and wrest from a tiny wave-washed shoal Canada's greatest known silver deposit.

Frue's first breakwaters proved mere toys against Superior's hurricane-like storms. Eventually Frue completed a wall strong enough to withstand any tempest, and he added bunkhouses and mine buildings. But during the next spring break-up a freak tidal wave loomed out of the dark waters, hurtling a wall of ice against the helpless wooden buildings.

Finally, by 1872, the mine was in full swing. On the mainland grew the miners' village, with a store, mill, log jail, and 50 sturdy homes. In just 12 years the mine yielded riches worth more than $3.5 million. But the wily lake had one more ruse. Because the shafts had crept outward under the floor of the lake, pumps were constantly chugging to keep leakage at bay. And with the surrounding forest now denuded of its wood supply, the town was dependent for its winter fuel upon the fall coal boat. But the ice of 1884 came early, stranding a surprised and some say inebriated coal boat captain in a distant harbour. Without fuel, the mine closed, the pumps fell silent, and the shafts filled with water. Sadly the miners packed their belongings and left the doomed mine.

But their sturdy homes did not long lie empty, for in nearby Fort William and Port Arthur the urban residents, deprived of their own waterfront by railway tracks and grain elevators, saw them as a tranquil recreational retreat. And that is how you find them today, at the end of provincial Highway 587, which winds its way south from the Trans-Canada Highway 11-17 through the scenic Sleeping Giant Provincial Park. Here, where the 50 houses, the one-time customs house, the weathered general store and the log jail gaze over Superior's waters, the permanent population now numbers only two. And on Superior's horizon lies the low, nearly imperceptible profile of a rocky shoal, now barren and wave washed, that once held the treasure trove of Canada's richest silver mine.

Silver Islet's century-old general store sits abandoned.

5
Ghost Railway to Nowhere

West of Thunder Bay a landscape of farmland gives way to one of lakes, rocks and forests. In these woods lies the most remote portion of the U.S. - Canada border to be found in Ontario. Yet it was the destination of one of northern Ontario's earliest railway ventures.

By the early 1880s Prince Arthur's Landing (later Port Arthur) had become a booming port. Rumours of rich iron deposits and sparkling silver veins were drawing miners, prospectors and investors into its mountainous hinterland. To tap this seemingly rich bonanza, a group of Port Arthur businessmen incorporated a railway company known best as the Port Arthur, Duluth & Western. It would, they proposed, travel through the silver fields and tap into the rich iron deposits just across the border in Minnesota. Its western terminus lay at Gunflint, Minnesota, deep in the woods.

The P.D. & W.'s Rosslyn station now guards only an abandoned right-of-way.

However, by the time the P.D. & W. opened in 1893, the silver market was in a depression and the string of small mines closed. By 1899 the railway had fallen into disuse and was acquired for a nominal sum by MacKenzie and Mann, who were then completing Canada's second great transcontinental line, the Canadian Northern. Although mildly interested in the resources along the line, their main interest was in avoiding duplication of the 18 miles of line into Thunder Bay that the P.D. & W. had already built.

Between 1904 and 1939 the old P.D. & W. was gradually dismantled as far as Twin City, where it now links with the present C.N.R. line to Sioux Lookout. Its nickname, "the Poverty, Distress and Welfare," aptly summed up its economic performance.

Today the hills and back roads southwest of Thunder Bay yet reveal the ghosts of the railway to nowhere. Just west of Stanley and south of the Trans-Canada Highway, a strangely solid iron bridge carries a dirt township road. This was the P.D. & W.'s mightiest bridge, over the wide Kaministikwia River. The overgrown roadbed appears and disappears along the township roads and through the bush. At Hymers an historical plaque commemorates the railway, while the odd orientation of the tiny main street in Nolalu reflects its construction along either side of the P.D. & W. track.

And in the shadow of Silver Mountain, once the site of a pair of busy silver-mining towns, there sits a large, solitary building. With its prominent gable and its bay window, it is the former Silver Mountain railway station.

Beyond that the roadbed gradually disappears into the remote bush and lakeland that straddle the Ontario - Minnesota border. It was and remains the ghost railway to nowhere.

6
Grand Canyon North

It's little wonder that Group of Seven painters A.Y. Jackson, Franklin Carmichael and Lauren Harris fell in love with Superior country. Nearly every bend in its rivers, nearly every bay in its lakes contains a panorama of mountain scenery that is as unexpected as it is awesome. And when at the end of a trail through a pine forest near Nipigon, Ontario, the land drops away at your feet unannounced to reveal a sudden and magnificent canyon, you understand how scenery can be called "unexpected."

As a tourist attraction Ouimet Canyon Provincial Park is little known. No motels have sprung up to accommodate the hoards, no gift shops line the roads. Most Trans-Canada Highway travellers simply ignore the simple brown sign that points the way. But as a visual spectacle Ouimet Canyon is breathtaking and unique.

Two hundred metres wide and 200 deep, the craggy crevice twists several kilometres north from the lip of the grand plateau into which it has been cut. Its sheer rocky walls resemble a row of pillars, some of which erosion has made free-standing. Deep in the gully, so little sunshine penetrates, that winter ice can linger into June and only hardy species of Arctic plants can survive.

The canyon traces its origins back to the last great ice age, when a sheet of ice two kilometres thick crept southward, scouring and gouging everything in its path. Here at Ouimet a tongue of ice crept down what started as a small gully, pushing rocks and boulders before it until it had bulldozed out a yawning canyon.

The road to Ouimet Canyon from the Trans-Canada Highway (about 55 kilometres east of Thunder Bay) passes some surprisingly lush farmland before twisting its way up the face of the rocky plateau. From the parking lot in the provincial park a trail winds through a pine forest up to the sudden and unfenced rim of the canyon. If you fear heights or worry about small kids, designated viewing areas do have guardrails around them. However the several trails that go through the park require sturdy hiking shoes and careful footing.

From the viewing areas the panorama encompasses not only the defile itself but also its rugged gates at the rim of the plateau, the forested lands beyond, and along the far horizon the grey waters of Lake Superior.

As you gaze at the results of nature's remarkable strength, as the northern stillness rings in your ears, and as the sharp pine-scented air stings your nostrils, you will understand why the Group of Seven kept coming back.

Ontario's miniature version of the Grand Canyon, Ouimet Canyon, is so deep and narrow that plants otherwise native to the Arctic thrive in its dark recesses.

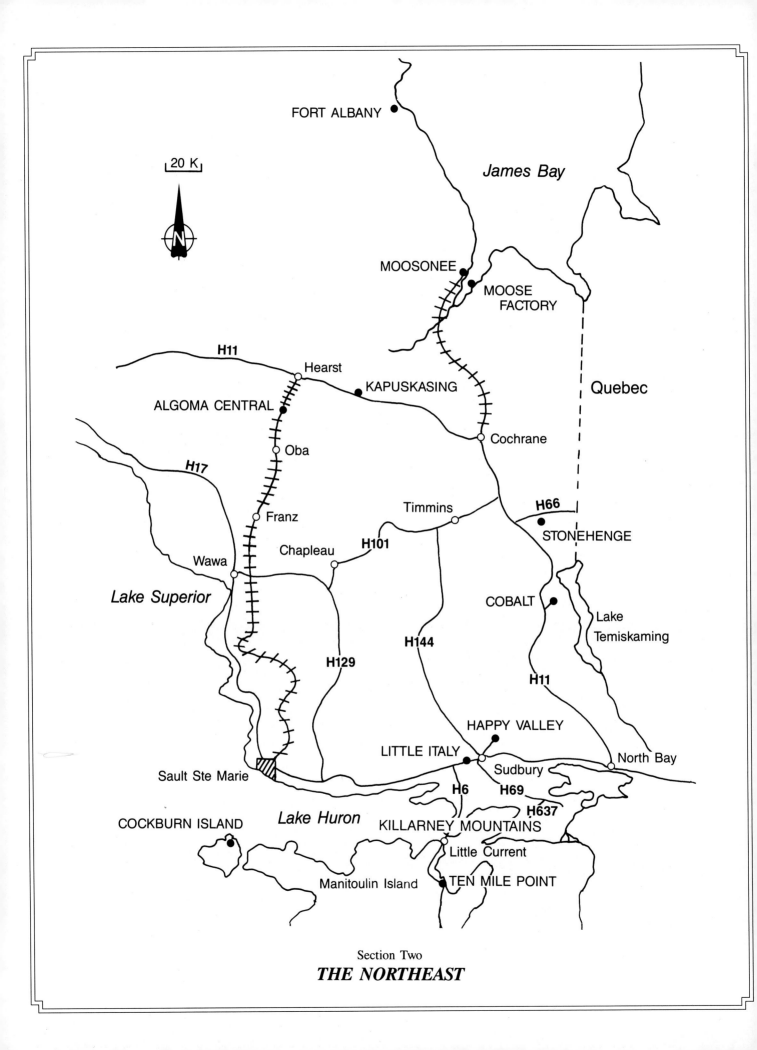

FORT ALBANY

James Bay

20 K

MOOSONEE

MOOSE
FACTORY

H11

Hearst

KAPUSKASING

Quebec

ALGOMA CENTRAL

Cochrane

Oba

H17

Timmins

H66

Franz

STONEHENGE

Chapleau

H101

Wawa

Lake Superior

COBALT

Lake
Temiskaming

H144

H11

H129

HAPPY VALLEY

LITTLE ITALY

North Bay

Sault Ste Marie

Sudbury

H6

H69

H637

COCKBURN ISLAND

Lake Huron

KILLARNEY MOUNTAINS

Little Current

Manitoulin Island

TEN MILE POINT

Section Two
THE NORTHEAST

7
Moosonee: On the Frontier Fringe

There still is a "frontier" in Ontario. It is called Moosonee. End of rail and as far north as you can go by public land transportation in Ontario, it is a rough-and-tumble town full of frontier spirit and appearance, and it is the gateway to Ontario's native northland.

The main street is a hodgepodge of old and new buildings, styled for utility not appearance, that straggle between the railway station at one end of the street and the Moose River landing at the other end. By the station a colourful chip wagon displays a menu in both Cree and English.

Originally a tiny Revillon Freres trading post, Moosonee boomed when the Temiskaming & Northern Ontario Railway (now the Ontario Northland) finished laying its most northerly rails in 1931. Although it is located on Arctic tidewater, the treacherous and shifting sand bars throughout the mouth of the Moose River dashed any hope of it ever becoming an ocean port.

In the middle of the Moose River, Moose Factory by contrast is Ontario's oldest English settlement. Here in 1672 Charles Bayly of the Hudson's Bay Company established that company's second trading post. After falling to the French in 1686 (a daring adventurer named de Troyes had travelled overland to surprise the fort in an attack from the rear) Moose Fort returned to the Company in 1713 and has traded continuously since 1730.

Several old trading-post buildings are preserved, including the former residence, St. Thomas' Anglican Church (1864), and what may be Ontario's oldest wooden structure, a blacksmith shop built in 1740. In the church — which like the blacksmith shop is open to the tourists — the stained-glass windows depict traditional northern native life, and the altar and liturgical vestments are made of moosehide.

Amid the modern federal-style houses of the natives, you will see many of the more traditional tepees.

In them the native women cook bannock (an unleavened bread cooked on a stick over a fire) for the tourists, while in the community hall the local church ladies' group provides refreshments. You may find conversation limited, however, for few of the Cree inhabitants are fluent in English. Access to Moose Factory is by water only. At the foot of the main street in Moosonee a fleet of native freight canoes waits to rush tourists across the shallow Moose River to the island.

If Moosonee and Moose Factory have only whetted your appetite for a taste of Ontario's native northland, you may continue up the James Bay coast on Air Creebec's "milk run." Departing Moosonee around midday, you will touch down in such outposts as Fort Albany, Kashechawan and Attawapiskat. Later in the afternoon you will return to Moosonee, where you may continue southbound the same day.

(Access is by Ontario Northland local or Polar Bear Express trains out of Cochrane, or by air from Cochrane or Timmins. Accommodation in Moosonee is limited, although the return Express from Cochrane allows you half a day to look around Moosonee and gets you back to Cochrane the same evening. Two Bay tours in Moosonee provide a guided bus tour of both Moosonee and Moose Factory.)

First Street as viewed from the station.

A Cobalt grocer built his store around an abandoned headframe to keep his meat and produce cool.

The size of Cobalt's railway station testifies to the importance Cobalt once held.

8
Cobalt's Boom-Town Legacy

When a pair of railway timber scouts named McKinley and Darraugh discovered silver by a tiny remote lake in northeastern Ontario in 1903, they couldn't have known that their find would change forever the landscape that surrounded them. The forest of pine that cooled them on that hot August day would soon be stripped bare to make way for a forest of mining headframes.

Shortly after the rails of the Temiskaming & Northern Ontario Railway reached the shores of that lake, a confusion of shacks and boom-town stores began to vie for space on the tumble of rocks beside it. The railway called it Cobalt. Almost overnight the forest vanished as miners clanged into the granite frantically grasping for the silver. They weren't disappointed. From the bedrock came boulders the size of sheds and veins the size of sidewalks. The trees were replaced by a forest of a different kind, one of headframes that at the peak of activity numbered 52.

Between 1908 and 1910 the name Cobalt echoed around the world and the town quickly grew to 10,000. But the great stock market crash of 1929 devastated the silver market and Cobalt became a ghost town.

Although Cobalt has rebounded to 2,000, you can find among the now silent hills the ghosts of its heyday. Simply follow the well-marked "Heritage Trail" at the western entrance to Cobalt (Highway 11B). This trail will guide you to gaping fissures that once contained the fabulous silver veins and past a ghostly forest of headframes, many with empty cabins and bunkhouses at their feet. Their names, once household words — Laurentian, University, Buffalo, Nipissing — are now utterly forgotten.

Cobalt boomed so quickly that there was no time for town planning. Streets ended abruptly at rock ridges, upon which a tumble of shacks, hotels and wooden stores were thrown together, while beneath the dusty streets half a dozen mines burrowed out a maze of shafts.

The mines are still now. Rusting headframes guard both the western and eastern approaches to the town. But in the centre of the one-time boom town stands the most unusual sight of all, a headframe which protrudes from the roof of a store. When the Coniagas Mine ceased operating in 1926, Anthony Giachino built a store around the headframe and used the cool air from the depths of the shaft to refrigerate his meat and vegetables. The store operated until the 1960s, when the Cobalt Area Restoration Office took it over.

Perhaps Cobalt's grandest building was its unusual station. To complement Cobalt's lofty new status as the cultural centre of New Ontario, the T. & N.O. commissioned John M. Lyle to design a station that would show off the T. & N.O. to the world.

Completed in 1909 the station was the grandest on the line and one of the most elegant in Ontario. With its beaux-arts lines and arched two-storey waiting room, the station was one of the town's largest buildings and one of the few made of brick. Now the station sits unused awaiting its uncertain fate at the hands of apparently disinterested municipal authorities.

Cobalt has been unusually rich in its boom-town heritage, with its headframes, the Fred Larose blacksmith shop (Larose found one of Cobalt's richest mines), its narrow winding streets that are remeniscent of Quebec City, Ontario's first provincial police lockup, its grand railway station and a half mile of boom-town stores. Sadly, much has fallen victim to fire and neglect. Local interest in preserving what remains, as Tombstone has so successfully done in Arizona, has never been keen. Now it is too late. Only a few reminders of Cobalt's fascinating history survive.

(A postscript: Cobalt's boom-town legacy took an ironic and potentially tragic turn in 1986. When a small pothole appeared on Highway 11B near the western end of town, residents thought little of it. But the pothole quickly grew until it became obvious that a forgotten mine shaft deep beneath the road was collapsing and taking a busy provincial highway with it. A concrete-and-steel support has arrested the collapse and the road has been restored. But as Cobalt residents walk and drive through their community, they must now wonder when another forgotten shaft will suddenly open at their feet.)

9

The Algoma Central: A Train Ride from the Past

As the first rays of sunrise brighten the faded insulbrick on the ancient Hearst railway station, bleary-eyed tourists begin to wander onto the platform. Awaiting them on the tracks, hissing and steaming, are the two passenger cars of the Algoma Central Railway's train #1, also known as the "Milk Run." They are about to embark on one of the last of the old-style train rides in North America.

Not a museum train, the A.C.R. is all utilitarian. The 476-kilometre line between the remote northern Ontario sawmill town of Hearst and the bustling industrial city of Sault Ste. Marie is populated by prospectors, loggers, trappers, cottagers and campers, all dependent on this train to link them with the "outside."

A.C.R. #1 operates on the traditional train order system rather than the newer and now almost universal one of computerized, centralized traffic control. Throughout its route it stops on demand. At Wabatong, a wooden "umbrella" station beside Wabatong Lake, cottagers and fishermen clamber on board. At Oba, a community of 100 still entirely dependent on rail access, parcels and freight are hand-loaded on or off the mail car while the passengers scurry into the nearby general store for a coffee. Oba is the A.C.R.'s junction with the Canadian National Railway's main line and a grand stuccoed two-storey station built in the Canadian Northern style testifies to this status.

Further down the line the village of Franz, at the junction with the Canadian Pacific main line, is much reduced from the size it was in its heyday. Here Ojibway children besiege the train, anxious to sell their current crop of blueberries, which proliferate in the area's sand flats. At Goudreau, a large station now stands empty, for, like the town beside it, it is just a ghost, a decaying remnant of the grander days when Goudreau was a busy gold-mining town.

The morning hours of the southbound are spent hurtling through a low spruce forest that is flat and dreary. But during the afternoon, spectacular cliffs loom above a foaming stream as the train enters the Agawa Canyon. This ancient and spectacular defile is the destination of the hugely popular tourist trains, the longest in the world, that depart daily from Sault Ste. Marie. But unlike the tourist trains, the milk run does not stop to allow for an afternoon of picnicking and hiking.

Throughout the trip, which can last up to ten hours, an easy joviality permeates the train. Tourists, usually American, crowd the rear platform to absorb a remoteness almost lost south of the border, while the conductors casually explain the features of the passing landscape. As cottagers, natives and trappers scramble on board at the many flag stops, acquaintances are renewed and familiar chatter fills the coaches.

Then by the time the train slows to wind past the suburbs and factories of Sault Ste. Marie, a weary silence descends. Finally the train hisses to a halt at the modern Sault station. Last farewells are heard and the empty train eases away from the platform to await the morning run.

Passenger trains of the future will be fast and modern. Computers will run the speed, the stops and the ticketing, much like air services. But as long as the trappers, the hunters and the loggers of Algoma require it, A.C.R. #1 will continue to be a train from the past.

A typical "umbrella" station in the remote bushland served by the ACR.

10
Cockburn Island: A Ghost Island Township

Ontario's Municipal Directory isn't exactly recommended bedtime reading, but on page 134 of the 1996 edition of this otherwise statistical tome, there is a number that makes the reader take notice.

Under the heading District of Manitoulin, Cockburn Island seems to have all the requirements of a normal incorporated Ontario municipality: it has a reeve, a treasurer, a clerk, a roads engineer, a municipal office and 84 assessed "households." The thing that makes it unusual is its population: 2.

That's not a misprint. Once home to a busy farming community, a small fishing fleet and a little village named Tolsmaville, all in all more than 300 people, Cockburn Island is now abandoned. However, because most of the properties are still used by the former residents as cottages in summer or as hunt camps in fall, the island retains its municipal status.

The story of Cockburn Island resembles those of its Lake Huron and Manitoulin Island shoreline neighbours. Glowing reports of forestry, fishing and farming drew a rush of settlers onto the island around 1880. Regular steamer service connected it with its waterbound neighbours and took its fish, lumber and crops to market. But while most of the other communities gradually acquired road or rail links to their neighbours and their markets, Cockburn Island remained entirely dependent upon its steamers. Despite its prosperity,

Cockburn Island never really boomed. In fact, after each of the world wars, many of those who had left to fight simply never returned. Its population declined slowly, until that sad day in 1963 when the steamer *Norgoma* chugged away from the Tolsmaville dock for the last time. The residents packed up their belongings and sadly moved across the North Channel to the mainland communities of Thessalon or Blind River. Even the municipal office was relocated to Massey.

As you approach the dock from the water, the village of Tolsmaville looks normal enough; frame houses built in the simple turn-of-the-century style line the dirt streets and a row of pickup trucks sits in a field by the wharf. But as you step ashore you see that many of the old houses sit empty and weathered, and the trucks are rusted and without licence plates (they are reserved for the short but active fall deer hunt). The farm fields have reverted to bush, and on the far side of the island the village in the small Indian Reserve is silent and overgrown. However, a few of the houses and other buildings, such as the church and the community hall, are kept painted and landscaped by their seasonal users, and along the shore of the harbour a few new cottages have appeared. But the peaceful yet haunting landscape that depicts the sad story of Cockburn Island, Ontario's ghost island township, is an image that will likely stay in your memory for quite some time.

The empty village of Tolsmaville on Cockburn Island, a ghost island township.

11
Sudbury's Little Italy

Ontario towns and villages tend to resemble each other. Surveying standards in the days of development dictated roads of 33-foot or 66-foot width, while residential lots were laid out first in uniform grids and later with somewhat more imagination on curving streets. While planned towns like Kapuskasing or Terrace Bay stand apart, all conform to the architectural and planning dictates of the day.

But tucked away in the former town of Copper Cliff, a company town constructed by the nickel-mining giant Inco, lies a hillside of houses, crammed together and jostling for position, reminiscent of an Italian mountainside community. The reason is simple — that is what it is.

In 1883 the construction of the C.P.R. suddenly flung open the vast mineral riches of the geological basin around what was then a small railway town named Sudbury Junction. Headframes, mills and smelter stacks began to appear on the rocky hilltops. The first was the Murray Mine, followed by the Canada Copper Company and Falconbridge, as well as a number of smaller companies. To avoid paying what would have been huge municipal taxes, the companies built their own towns, and in 1890 Copper Cliff was created by Canada Copper (later Inco).

West of Sudbury, beneath Inco's looming smelter and growing slag heaps, Inco built Copper Cliff's wide streets, its neat company houses, its stores and churches. But on a vacant rocky hilltop mere metres from the belching chimneys, a group of Italian miners decided to build their own houses. With no preplanned streets or lots to follow, they built in the rural Italian style to which they were accustomed. Their strong sense of community meant proximity to each other outweighed the desire for privacy or large lots. They built their houses in whatever shape, size or orientation suited them. Little space was left for yards, even less for streets, for at the time none owned cars.

The result is a scene almost from an Italian postcard. Narrow streets twist around the houses, while the houses squeeze each other at every angle. Although the homes are now individually owned, the area has remained resolutely Italian. Italian clubs and language dominate. Only metres from the nearest houses, Inco's superstack soars a half kilometre into the sky, belching sulphur-laden smoke. It is a symbol which may turn many away from the area, but 70 years ago the smelter meant jobs for a community of Italian miners and drew them almost as if in reverence to huddle at its feet.

Taste of the Appenines. Little Italy, an Italian enclave within Sudbury's Copper Cliff townsite, was built by Italian migrant miners to resemble their native mountainside villages.

12
Happy Valley and the Hill of Fire

In 1968 American moonwalkers Buzz Aldrin and Neil Armstrong prepared for man's first stroll on a foreign space body by practising on the scarred rocky ridges of Sudbury, Ontario (much to the chagrin of local residents). Burnt bare of vegetation and soil by the searing sulphur-laden smoke from the stacks of the nickel smelters, the land around this otherwise attractive city does resemble the moon.

The Sudbury Basin is a geological feature rich in nickel. At a time when the mineral meant jobs and wealth for the country, and when the dangers of pollution were not widely acknowledged, the smelters of Sudbury belched forth their untreated pollutants. Vegetation burned black and died, soil washed away and lakes turned into vinegar. Despite the awful devastation, six decades would pass before the voices of concern were finally heeded.

One pollution monitor was placed in the community of Happy Valley, where a hundred or so miners and their families lived in a small saucer-shaped valley beside the smoky smelter town of Falconbridge, northeast of Sudbury. Instances of illness and death from lung cancer seemed unusually high and the monitors confirmed what the residents had long suspected: death due to pollution. Sulphur-laden smog from the Falconbridge stacks that tower beside the valley rim often became trapped in the valley during times of temperature inversion. The toll was so devastating that the local and provincial governments joined with Falconbridge to move the residents out. This unusual exodus became the only evacuation in Canada to be caused by pollution.

By 1975 most were gone and the valley today is a silent testimony to the dangers that man has wrought upon himself. Void of any growth. Happy Valley's yellow and barren landscape evokes the deserts of Arizona. Like an oasis in the middle, a handful of stunted trees still guard a trio of empty houses, rusting cars and debris, while around the valley the black ridges of the Sudbury basin, burnt and treeless, stretch to the horizon.

Dusk's blue curtain has just settled over the western sky when suddenly a bright orange glow erupts from a dark hillside. It is followed quickly by another, then by another, as if a volcano has suddenly come to life. The glowing hillside then turns dark. Cars rev their motors simultaneously and disappear down the darkened road. Another slag-pouring at Inco's Cooper Cliff smelter in Sudbury has finished and the satisfied onlookers have departed the viewing area for their homes or motels.

Construction of the C.P.R. in 1883 revealed spectacular nickel mineralization among the rock ridges that ringed what was then a fledgling frontier town named Sudbury. Soon mines and headframes appeared on the hilly horizons. In December 1888 one of the first smelters was blown in by the Canada Copper Company (the word "nickel" didn't make its way into the company name until 1916, when it was renamed the International Nickel Company of Canada, today's Inco).

While not a glamour metal like gold or silver, nickel is particularly prized for its durability and resistance to corrosion. In order to extract the nickel, the ore must first be crushed and the nickel-bearing sulphides floated out. The concentrate is then smelted to produce nickel matte, which is refined into nickel products. The slag is what remains after the nickel has been melted out. While it is still red hot, the slag is poured into hopper cars, 15 at a time, and hauled by an electric engine to the top of a mound known as a slag heap. There, the cars are tipped and the glowing tongues of molten slag creep down the side of the heap. So spectacular is this sight that it has long been a popular attraction for Sudbury-area residents and visitors alike.

To complete the Sudbury mining experience you may also visit the Big Nickel Mine, on the same road, for a simulated underground tour of a mine operation, or popular Science North. Nothing will remain more vividly in your memory than the sight of that hillside on fire.

13
The White Crests of Killarney

Driving west on Highway 637 just south of Sudbury, you soon see the domes of white gleaming above the low green forest. Your first thought is that some freak of nature has preserved a mountain of snow into the summer season. But as you drive closer you realize that these are the legendary Lacloche Mountains of Killarney and the "snow" is quartzite rock of pure white.

Countless millions of years ago an ancient sea laid down a bed of sand that was unusually rich in silica. As the shifting bedrock hurled the seabed into a giant mountain range, the layers of silica were compressed into layers of white quartzite. Eons of rain, wind and grinding glaciers then eroded the lofty peaks into the round white knobs that today provide the spectacular backdrop to these northern shores of Georgian Bay and Lake Huron.

The area's early history has little to do with the scenery. Following the days when Killarney was a stopover for native and French-Canadian fur traders, logging companies began to strip the pine from the mountainsides. One of the earliest mills was that at Collins Inlet, 25 kilometres east of Killarney. A few company buildings yet survive and have been incorporated into a fishing camp.

The most important economic mineral hidden in the mountains was silica, used in glass-making. A one-time mine at Killarney Quarry, opposite the current village, is now a ghost town, while on nearby Badgely Island giant machines continue to tear into the white rocky domes. Recent proposals to quarry other of the more beautiful peaks have justly aroused a storm of protest.

But it was the scenery that attracted the area's earliest tourists. Among them were a pair of young painters named Franklin Carmichael and A.Y. Jackson, whose works "Summer Storm," "Bay of Islands" and "Nellie Lake" have become among the most prized Group of Seven works.

The pure white quartzite rocks of the Killarney mountains resemble a hillside of snow.

There are several ways you can follow their footsteps. Within the Killarney Provincial Park, one of the province's most popular, you can canoe the remote lakes or hike the lofty peaks. You can launch your boat into Georgian Bay at Killarney and explore the mountainbound Killarney Bay or Baie Fine. Or you can stay in your car and follow Highway 6 south from Espanola to lookouts on the Willis-ville Road or at Dreamers Rock (an ancient Indian meditation point, Dreamers Rock is still so sacred that you must obtain special permission from the Whitefish Indian band to visit it). But regardless of your means of conveyance, the Lacloche Mountains of Killarney remain one of the most unusual alpine destinations east of the Rockies.

14
A Viewpoint with a Difference

Despite its rolling, often hilly topography, Ontario is seldom considered a land of mountains and spectacular vistas. Yet beside one of the province's busiest highways, Manitoulin Island offers one of Canada's most spectacular viewpoints. The reason lies in an unusual combination of mountains, cliffs and island-studded waters.

The backbone and northern coast of the Manitoulin is the mighty Niagara Escarpment. Here it towers 100 - 150 metres above the land. But it is 15 kilometres south of the busy tourist town of Little Current on provincial Highway 6 that the Escarpment bends from north to west and creates a high promontory with a sweeping vista. It is known as Ten Mile Point Lookout. Lapping at the foot of the promontory are the waves of northern Lake Huron as they funnel into the North Channel between the island and the mainland. And providing the backdrop is the white quartzite spine of the Lacloche Mountains.

The result is one of the most sweeping, breathtaking views that Ontario offers.

Because so many travellers pause to take in the scenery, the Ministry of Transportation has provided parking, picnic, and washroom facilities. Beside the lookout a gift shop offers souvenirs of Canada, "made-in-Quebec" Indian moccasins and other trinkets.

There are only two ways to reach Ten Mile Point Lookout, by driving south on Highway 6 from the Trans-Canada (Highway 17) at Espanola, or by embarking upon the car ferry *Chee-Chimaun* at Tobermory and then following Highway 6 northward from its terminus at South Baymouth. If using the latter, reserve well ahead for both ferry and motel space.

Manitoulin Island's Ten Mile Point view is one of Ontario's most spectacular.

15
Stonehenge Ontario?

Don't try telling the folks around Larder Lake that Ontario doesn't have its own "Stonehenge."

While the unusual aggregation of 18 huge boulders — some twice the height of a man — in the bushland on the north shore of Larder Lake may not replicate the dramatic visual impact of the Stonehenge formation on England's stark Salisbury plain, its strange alignments do raise some questions.

How did the giant boulders get there? There are simply too many huge boulders in a small area, two hectares, for the great glaciers to have randomly deposited them. And why do their alignments match exactly with the rising and setting of the sun on the summer and winter solstices? And can their proximity to Mt. Cheminis, a huge volcanic plug that dominates the landscape 20 kilometres to the east and which was once a prehistoric native shrine, be simply a coincidence?

Perhaps one of the clues lies in the most recent interpretation of the de Troyes diary. Pierre de Troyes was a French soldier who in 1686 travelled overland from the St. Lawrence to surprise the British garrison at Moose Fort on James Bay. To make his way through the mysterious Ontario bushland de Troyes followed ancient Indian routes. A recent reinterpretation of his diary places the main route not to the east, as previously assumed, but along Larder Lake and right past the mystery boulders.

Other clues include results of nearby archaeological digs that place the Indians' presence at more than 6,000 years, and a field of jagged rocks that may represent an ancient Indian quarry. Together the clues point to the possibility that here in northeastern Ontario lies a major and hitherto undetected centre of prehistoric Indian worship.

Because the boulders have so long been hidden by the bush and their alignments never before taken, archaeologists are only now beginning to investigate. Are they truly a prehistoric "Stonehenge" or simply a random arrangement? The archaeologists will soon tell us. Until then, what is more fun than a mystery?

Because the rocks must be protected from interference until security is established, those who wish to visit the site should inquire locally in the town of Larder Lake for directions.

Four boulders in a line on the shore of Larder Lake.

16
Kapuskasing: A Planned Town in the Northern Bush

West of Cochrane, in northeastern Ontario, Highway 11 lies straight and flat, flanked on one side by abandoned farmland, on the other by a single lonely railway track. A short distance north a low woodland stretches unbroken to the Arctic. It is, in other words, the least likely place to find Ontario's first modern "planned" town.

Kapuskasing began innocuously as MacPherson Siding in 1913 on the newly completed National Transcontinental/Grand Trunk Pacific Railway. Its isolation made it ideal for a prisoner of war camp during the First World War. Following the war, returning soldiers were directed to what was touted as "New Ontario," where the flat, stonefree soils of the Great Clay Belt of northeastern Ontario would spawn a prosperous new agricultural

Inn (right) and municipal office overlooking a bay in the Kapuskasing River.

community. But even an agricultural experimental farm could not overcome the harsh climate and unrelenting flies, and most of the fledgling farmers returned south.

Had it not been for the Kapuskasing Pulp and Timber Company, that might have been the end of the settlement. However the water power of the falls in the Kapuskasing River and the level terrain on the river bank convinced the company to locate its mill and workers here. Anxious to justify their interest in the new north, the Ontario government undertook to build the company a new town and it was to be the best. It would be a planned town, a model for future northern towns, and would contain gardens, Tudor architecture, and streets that would radiate from a central circle.

By 1923 Kapuskasing, with its new brick railway station, was complete. The Kapuskasing Inn, with its grand Tudor gables, and the recreation centre (later the town hall) gazed over the landscaped banks of a bay in the river, while the equally grand hospital dominated a triangular green common. Businesses grouped around the circle in the centre of town, while stately homes flanked the curving streets.

In 65 years Kapuskasing has changed modestly. Although highway businesses now stretch out along Highway 11, the circle remains the heart of the community, dominated now by a symbolic "K" added in recent years. Former shanty towns that clung to its fringes have been incorporated and upgraded. Despite the busy traffic on the highway, passenger trains still depart the station daily for Cochrane and Toronto.

For all the changes, Kapuskasing, surrounded by the remains of a failed farming scheme, by faded railway towns and by seemingly endless bushland, remains the anomaly of the North.

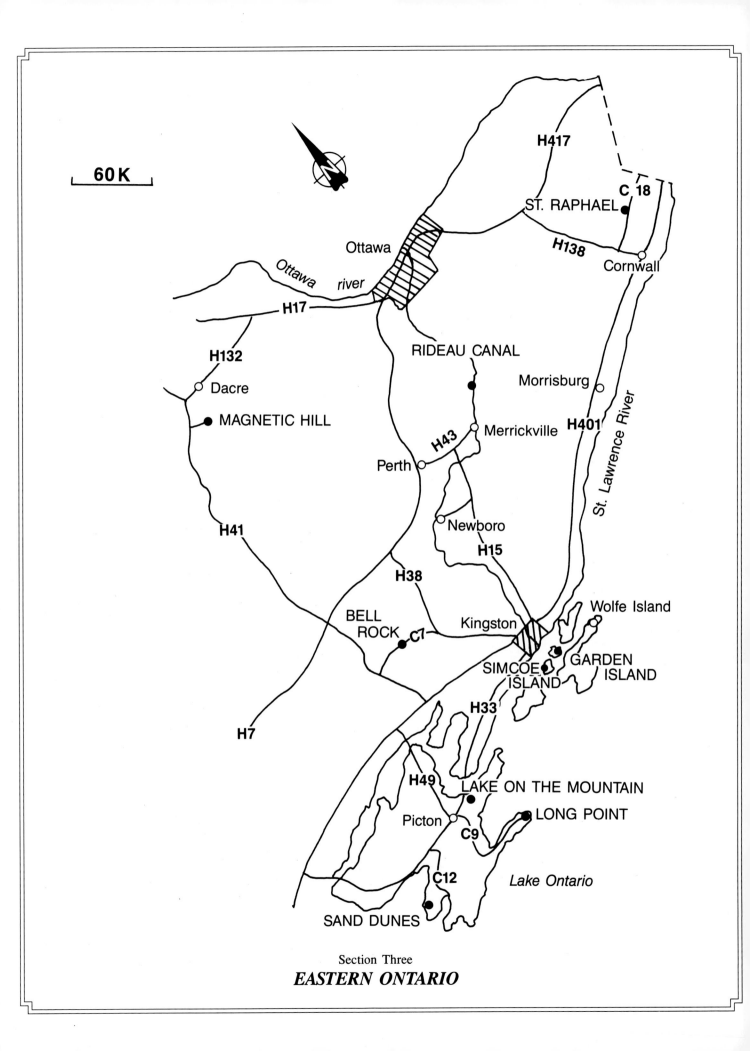

60 K

H417

C 18

ST. RAPHAEL

H138

Cornwall

Ottawa

Ottawa river

H17

RIDEAU CANAL

Morrisburg

St. Lawrence River

H132

Dacre

MAGNETIC HILL

H43

Merrickville

H401

Perth

H41

Newboro

H15

H38

Kingston

Wolfe Island

BELL ROCK

C7

SIMCOE ISLAND

GARDEN ISLAND

H7

H33

H49

LAKE ON THE MOUNTAIN

Picton

LONG POINT

C9

C12

Lake Ontario

SAND DUNES

Section Three
EASTERN ONTARIO

17
The Ruins of St. Raphael

Ruins romantic and picturesque are more associated with Europe than with North America. Here ruins tend to be of factories and mills, harsh forms that reflect our obsession with industry rather than beauty. But the ruins of the magnificent St. Raphael cathedral on County Road 18, 40 kilometres northeast of Cornwall, contain the history, romance and grace that one would more closely identify with Greece or Rome.

In 1784 the Revolutionary War in the United States was over, and in return for their loyalty and courage, those who fought for England were rewarded with land grants in what would become Ontario.

After trooping wearily behind their commander, Sir John Johnson, the officers and men of the 1st Battalion, King's Royal Regiment of New York, most of Highland Scots origin, finally arrived on the banks of the Raisin River. Here, in eastern Ontario's Charlottenburg Township, their land grants, swampy and forested, awaited them.

Two years later 500 more Scots arrived direct from the Highlands led by their parish priest, Alexander MacDonnell. (Most Highland Scots follow the Roman Catholic faith.) The parish grew quickly and prospered.

The first father MacDonnell died in 1803 and was replaced by another priest of the same name. Putting all the tenacity of his heritage behind him, MacDonnell succeeded in making his parish, which he called St. Raphael, the administrative centre of the Catholic church in Upper Canada. In 1821 he began construction of a magnificent stone cathedral to match the status of his parish. Five years later he added the Iona Seminary.

For a century and a half the cathedral dominated the rolling farmlands from its hilltop perch. Then, in 1970, fire roared through the church. Flames lashed out through the windows as the roof collapsed in a whirl of sparks.

But again the tenacity of their roots came to the fore, bolstered now by the infusion of French-Canadian Catholics, and the parishioners decided the ruin should neither be demolished nor replaced but rather remain a ruin, as if to commemorate this act of God.

Now landscaped, the ruin is still the focus of the parish. Services and plays now occur under a roofless sky. The first-time visitor to the ruins of St. Raphael must pause to remind himself that he is not in Greece but in Ontario.

The picturesque ruins of St. Raphael cathedral.

18
Garden Island

Ontario's history enthusiasts are indeed fortunate in the many pioneer villages they may visit. Upper Canada Village, Black Creek Pioneer Village, Lang and Doon pioneer villages are a few of the many sites to which historical buildings have been relocated. Old Fort William and Ste. Marie Among the Hurons are detailed replications of villages that have long vanished. The only 19th-century pioneer village that might have more appeal is one that remains unaltered and on site. And Garden Island fills that bill.

In 1836 Hiram Cook and Dileno Dexter Calvin decided that the tiny limestone Garden Island at the outlet of Lake Ontario into the St. Lawrence River was just what they were looking for. Because the Great Lakes were than a pioneer lumber producer, the two entrepreneurs began an oak stave shipping business on the island. Its proximity to Kingston and its situation at the exit of the lakes made the location ideal. Their business quickly evolved into shipbuilding, and by the end of the century they had launched nearly two dozen vessels. The population swelled to 700 and the village became an incorporated municipality. But the need for larger steel-hulled ships and the proliferation of the railroads doomed the operation and Garden Island fell silent.

Today you can still see the many 19th-century buildings associated with the shipbuilding: the sail loft, Calvin's white mansion, simple workers' cabins and the beautiful two-storey wooden company office. Now the seasonal properties of many Kingston residents, they are lovingly maintained, little altered in their 19th-century style. A living pioneer village.

Up until a few years ago the Wolfe Islander free ferry, which links Kingston with Wolfe Island, called regularly. No longer. Now you must make your own way there. The island lies about one kilometre off Wolfe Island, three from Kingston. In either place you may inquire about renting a small boat to take you there. The natives are friendly if you respect their town.

Garden Island, once a busy shipbuilding community, is now an unusual cottage settlement.

19
Ontario's Smallest Ferry

As Ontarians hurl their cars along highways 401, 427 or 403, few pause to consider the more leisurely pace of a ferry. Many have tried the popular *Chee Chimaun*, which swallows 115 cars at a time and glides them across Georgian Bay. Few, however, realize that Ontario claims no fewer than 16 car ferry services, nearly all of them free. Three ferry services cross each of the Ottawa and St. Clair rivers, a pair are for island Indian reserves, while Canada's southernmost ferry links mainland Ontario with Pelee Island, Canada's most southerly point of land. But the greatest concentration lies near Kingston.

Here at the entrance to the St. Lawrence River a handful of large, flat islands attracted early pioneer settlers. Although the populations have subsequently declined, the islands remain occupied and are connected to the mainland by ferry. The largest of the five, the *Wolfe Islander* III, carries more than 50 cars and trucks to busy Wolfe Island. While others link Howe Island and Amherst Island to the mainland, the smallest of all is the two-car cable ferry to Simcoe Island.

Announced only by a small green sign the landing is nothing more than a beach. Here the little ferry grinds against the sand and unceremoniously plunks down its gangway. Because it links Simcoe Island only to Wolfe Island and not to the mainland the ferry coincides its schedule with that of the *Wolfe Islander* III.

Once home to more than a dozen farm families, Simcoe Island is now more popular for cottaging and only a pair of farms survive. At the far western end of the island an historic lighthouse provides a remote destination for picnickers.

Although only one of 16 ferries that ply Ontario's waters, the Simcoe Island ferry is the smallest and takes you on an unusual excursion to a place where cars are an anomaly rather than the norm.

The Simcoe Island ferry is one of Ontario's smallest and least-known ferry services.

20
Lake on the Mountain

At first glance it looks natural enough, a little lake sparkling in the sun, surrounded by willow trees. But then you look behind you, and there, 100 metres below, at the foot of a limestone cliff, spreads Lake Ontario's Bay of Quinte. Then it begins to sink in. The little lake is sitting on the brink of a cliff, with no outlet and no apparent source.

Located in Prince Edward County, seven kilometres from the town of Picton, the lake long puzzled geologists. How did it get there? Why has it stayed there? Until just a few years ago no one even knew how deep it was. Then, as they explored its depths, geologists learned that it was spring fed and about 60 metres deep. But just as they were solving some of these puzzles, the scientists uncovered another, even more intriguing mystery. The fluctuation in the water level of the lake seemed to coincide with those occurring on Lake Erie, more than 200 kilometres away and with no direct connection. Is there a mysterious underground network of rivers that links Lake Erie with the Lake on the Mountain? Or do the strange fluctuations relate to some other unusual factor?

The attractions around the lake are numerous and don't have a lot to do with its mysteries. A small park beside the lake provides an environment for picnicking and hiking, while across the road a lofty viewpoint offers vistas of the Bay of Quinte, the mainland shore and the free Glenora ferries that shuttle back and forth carrying Highway 33 traffic. Van Alstine's old stone store, which dates from the days of the Loyalists, sits empty beside the park, while at the foot of the cliff the several buildings that comprise the Glenora mill complex date among the oldest stone mill buildings in the province. But all attention focuses upon the Lake on the Mountain. It has been a mystery since it was discovered and it will likely remain a mystery for years to come.

Picton's mysterious Lake on the Mountain lurks near the lip of the cliff that overlooks the Glenora mill.

21
The Other Long Point

In 1889 Thomas Murray blasted away the limestone bedrock that had connected Prince Edward County with mainland Ontario. As the water surged through the channel that would become the Murray Canal, Prince Edward County became an island.

Except for an early version of the Danforth Road that crossed the county, linking pioneer York (now Toronto) with Kingston, mainland Ontario has passed Prince Edward by. Main roads and railways all follow the mainland shore, leaving the county a relative backwater — to some a welcome one. And the quietest part of all is the long neck of land that stretches far out into Lake Ontario and is known as Long Point (not to be confused with the better-known Long Point on Lake Erie). At the tip of that point lies perhaps Ontario's best-kept secret, the cove at Point Traverse. Here a placid little lagoon surrounded by willows is home to Lake Ontario's last commercial fishing fleet. Cabins, icehouses and net racks crowd the shoreline, while just beyond the gravel bar that

guards the entrance lies the vast and sometimes furious Lake Ontario. An ancient wooden lighthouse, painted the mandatory red and white, warns ships away from the treacherous rocks that lurk beneath the shallow waters off the point.

A tranquil County Road 7 winds its way to Long Point from Highway 33 near the historic county town of Picton. Along the way, at South Bay, you may visit a stone lighthouse (relocated here from the distant Duck Islands) and see the maritime artifacts in the adjacent museum, or see the ruins of the nearby ghost town of Port Milford (about two kilometres east of South Bay on County Road 13).

Then, as houses become fewer and traffic nearly nonexistent, you realize that you are leaving behind the noise and bustle of busy southern Ontario. First you pass through a federal wildlife reserve, then by a string of low limestone cliffs with beaches of white boulders at their feet, until finally, 30 kilometres from Picton, you enter the little cove. If it seems you have entered a different world, in many ways you have.

Lake Ontario's last commercial fishing colony, at Long Point, is remote and tranquil.

22
The Dune That Ate a Town

Although it didn't exactly "eat" a town, a giant wall of sand moved across Prince Edward County between 1890 and 1920 to consume a sizable settlement before finally being halted. And it was all due to beer.

The civil war that tore apart the United States during the early 1860s had considerable impact on Canada. When the U.S. government slapped a surtax on whisky, American consumers switched to beer. And the best barley for beer was considered to be Canadian.

Canadian farmers hurriedly turned all available fields to barley production. But Prince Edward County, with its mild climate and its close proximity to U.S. ports just across Lake Ontario, became Ontario's major barley producer.

Cattle were hustled off their pastures and onto the most marginal lands in the county, the dunes. Following the retreat of the last glaciers, the Prince Edward peninsula had acted to block Lake Ontario's eastward currents and built up a long beach of sand. Over the centuries the prevailing winds whipped the sand into a ridge of dunes that measured 8 kilometres long, 2 kilometres wide and 50 metres high. Over time, a mat of grass and shrubs stabilized the dunes. But once the cattle started to roam the dunes, eating away the fragile cover, the dunes grew restless and started once more to move.

Slowly at first, then with increasing determination, the dunes moved inland. Fields, fences and then outbuildings and barns soon disappeared under the moving white wall. The West Bay Road had to be realigned a number of times to avoid being consumed. The advancing dunes spared nothing. A brick factory stood stubbornly in the path of the dunes until wind-whipped sand finally forced the owners to dismantle the plant and flee. Even the popular Evergreen Lodge failed to withstand the onslaught and was dismantled.

Desperate, the farmers planted willows on the dunes, but these had little effect. Finally, after the first war had ended, a reluctant Ontario government established a tree nursery on the dunes. As roots and branches grabbed the blowing sand, the dunes slowed and stopped.

Today, on the south shore of West Lake, both in and near the popular Sand Banks Provincial Park, you can see the evidence of the dunes' onslaught. The once straight West Lake Road bends and twists, contorted to avoid the advancing dunes. Cedar trees, once buried and later exposed, show double sets of roots, while relics of the pioneer brick factory yet litter its ill-fated site.

But the dunes haven't stopped entirely. Although they no longer advance across the countryside, the winds yet whip the sand into West Lake. Eventually the dunes that ate a sizable settlement will claim the lake and turn it into little more than a pond. The appetite of the dunes is insatiable.

Dunes at West Lake

23
Bell Rock Water-Powered Sawmill

A century and a half ago nearly every gully in Ontario that contained a trickle of water boasted sawmills, for as pioneers cut their trees and built their houses and barns, no industry was more urgently needed.

For several decades Ontario was a leading lumber producer. Then, by about 1880, when most of the forests had been cleared, not only were there no more logs for the mills, but also no more forest cover to regulate the water flows in the little gullies. In summer the creek beds were baked dry, while in the spring uncontrolled run-offs carried away mill dams and mills alike. Only on the larger rivers in the rocky Canadian Shield country did sawmilling retain a precarious fingerhold.

Far in the forested frontier of Frontenac County, the giant Rathbun Lumber Company controlled nearly four million acres of timber to feed its sawmills throughout eastern Ontario. One stood at Bell Rock, where the foaming waters of the Napanee River had enough power for a second sawmill as well as flour and carding mills.

And on the village streets the industries supported several stores and hotels.

But lumbering gradually declined and the mills closed. The stores and hotels vanished. There was, however, enough forested land, too rocky for farmers, to keep one of the sawmills going.

It is still going and may soon be the last water-powered sawmill to operate in Ontario. The present mill was built in 1920 and has in its life housed flour, veneer and planing mills. It has retained its original role as a vital local industry. Farmers from around Frontenac and neighbouring counties continue to bring their logs. It also contains a shingle and planing mill as well as the sawmill, and the flour and grist mill portions have been restored as a living museum.

The mill, off County Road 7, about 40 kilometres northwest of Kingston, is open seasonally to the public. You may take a guided tour to hear the rushing waters and the groaning gears, the once-familiar sound of a time when water was king.

The water-powered sawmill at Bell Rock still serves the area's farmers.

24
Waterway from the Past

In 1826 the Duke of Wellington was a legend, the hero of a determined campaign against another hero, Napoleon Bonaparte. His Peninsular campaign done, Wellington's military mind looked to Upper Canada, where memories of the 1812 war with the Americans were still fresh. Wary that the major transportation corridor, the St. Lawrence, lay perilously close to the U.S. border (in part it forms the boundary), Wellington proposed a canal that would link Kingston on Lake Ontario with a remote location on the Ottawa River and would be well away from possible American actions.

To carry out the difficult job he coaxed his former co-campaigner Colonel John By out of retirement. For five years 2,000 men sweated in eastern Ontario's malarial swamplands, hacking bush, trenching channels and hauling huge limestone blocks for the 50 dams and the 47 locks. In 1832 By's 200-kilometre waterway opened for traffic, a remarkable feat given the remoteness and total lack of mechanical assistance. But By did not return home a hero. Instead he was court-martialed for being over budget (a means of budget control which if used today would severely deplete the ranks of Canada's modern military). Not only that, but the Americans remained benign and the canal never served its military role. Prior to the railways it provided a key commercial link for the many little mill towns along it. Then it faded, until the 1950s and 60s, when recreational boating boomed.

But the canal is famed not for its pleasure boating, but for the fact that it remains historically intact right down to the hand operation of its locks and swing bridges. In fact, in a rare gesture of heritage preservation, the federal government placed the canal operation in the hands of Parks Canada and has identified it as an historical monument.

Indeed it is Canada's oldest and least-altered heritage "highway." By's military blockhouses still stand at Kingston Mills, Newboro and Merrickville, and at Jones Falls are the powder magazine and the world's highest stone dam of its day. At most locks Parks Canada attendants crank open the great stone gates of the locks by hand, as their predecessors have for a century and a half, while at the Narrows locks near Newboro even a swing bridge is cranked open by hand. The Scottish stonemasons who toiled to construct the stone walls and locks have left a lasting legacy in the beautiful stone stores and houses of Perth, Merrickville, and Kingston.

By may have died a broken man a century and a half ago, but even he would have been astonished at the durability of his legacy.

Locks on the Rideau Canal are still operated by hand.

Opposite:
Colonel John By built these triple locks at Jones Falls when eastern Ontario was little more than a malarial swamp.

25
Going Backwards Up a Hill

Ever get that feeling that for every step forward you are taking two backward? Try that in a car.

Specifically, try it on something called a "magnetic hill." You stop your car, turn off the ignition and wonder when you will start rolling forward down that hill in front of you. Instead you start rolling backward "up" the hill, or so it seems.

Just such a mysterious hill is located beside Highway 41, a few kilometres west of its intersection with Highway 132, in the remote reaches of Renfrew County.

What is the mysterious force pulling you up that hill? A strange magnetic ore body that tugs at metal objects? A freak wind tunnel effect? Neither. It is simply an optical illusion. It occurs when the configuration of a road and the surrounding hills gives you the appearance that you are on downhill grade when in fact you are facing an up grade.

The Black Donald mountains, which loom over southern Renfrew and Frontenac counties, and which give eastern Ontario some of its most spectacular scenery, contain many hidden valleys. And here, where Highway 41 winds its way up one of these gullies, the appearance is one of descent. The "hill" itself is located on a former alignment of the highway, just a few metres from the present highway. A small sign points the way.

Now you know the secret. But if you're taking your family or friends, don't tell them beforehand.

Incidently, as you will read in other entries, this area also offers some unusual scenic drives, ghost-town adventures and historic treasures. It's a great area in which to linger.

One of the mountain passes in the Black Donald Mountains contains the optical illusion known as a "magnetic hill."

26

The Teaching Rocks: Peterborough's Petroglyphs

The hollow echo of water gurgling beneath the rocks at their feet made the two young geologists uneasy. There, in the stillness of the forest north of Stony Lake, they felt as if they had entered a hallowed place. As they swept the moss away in their search for white crystalline limestone, something caught their eye, something odd. The surface of the rock was not smooth, as it should have been. Rather it contained strange etchings, thousands of them. Although they did not know it on that day in May 1954, the two men had uncovered one of North America's largest and most mysterious Indian petroglyphs, the Teaching Rocks.

Like the Bible of Jewish and Christian cultures, the Teaching Rocks recount the aboriginal story of life. As each young male entered adolescence, the elders of the tribe would lead him to this site, guided by the sound of the waterfalls and special guide rocks. One lesson at a time the elders taught the youngsters the meaning of life, as the Ojibway understood it and as the Teaching Rocks revealed it. The medicine wheel told them that life began as the sunrise in the east. Midday represented mid-life. The west meant old age, while the north referred to the afterlife. The spirits portrayed in the carvings taught that man must co-exist with nature.

After each lesson finished, the elders would cover the stones with moss to preserve the carvings from erosion. Today they are protected by a shelter in Petroglyph Provincial Park, 40 kilometres northeast of Peterborough near Highway 28. Here you may wonder at the strange shapes and possibly apply your own interpretations. Then you can watch the Ministry of Natural Resources' 20-minute award-winning film, *The Teaching Rocks*. Prepared by Lloyd Walton of that ministry, the film reveals the mysteries as told and narrated by the Ojibway themselves.

As you walk back to your car through the woods, you look around you and see nature through different eyes, and wonder why North America's European "conquerors" have run roughshod over the nature that the natives so easily co-existed with. It's a lesson that may now be too late to learn.

The mysteries of the native etchings in Petroglyph Provincial Park have recently been solved, in an award-winning movie, The Teaching Rocks, *produced by Ontario's Ministry of Natural Resources.*

27
The Last Giants

There they brood, from their lofty heights in the remote and rocky highlands of eastern Haliburton. Casting their shadows over the spindly forest at their feet, they are the lonely monarchs of the forest, the last of the giant white pines.

A century ago giant white pines were not unusual. In fact the great trees were so plentiful that the first settlers considered them a nuisance and burned them. Then, in 1810, with the dreaded Napoleon blockading Britain's timber suppliers around the Baltic Sea, Britain turned to the forests of Canada to supply her navy with masts.

With the inducement of duty-free entry to England, Canada's lumbermen pounced with zeal upon the great pine forests of the Ottawa Valley, a valley that penetrated far into the lush stands and at the same time provided easy water transportation to the ocean port of Montreal.

In 1854 a reciprocity treaty with the United States opened the booming American market to saw logs. With the Ottawa Valley now nearly stripped, lumber baron J.R. Booth cast his eager eyes upon the thick pine stands in what would become Algonquin Park. Like a wind-driven forest fire, Booth and other lumber barons raced across the highlands of central Ontario and within four decades had stripped the forests bare and created a Dante-esque landscape of burnt stumps and blackened rock.

How a pocket of several dozen giant pines in eastern Haliburton survived the onslaught remains a mystery. Perhaps the terrain was too rugged or the scheduled logging season too hostile. For whatever reason, the giants were spared.

Of the great pine forest that once covered Ontario's southern portions, these alone survive. More than 200 years old, they soar 50 metres into the sky and are so broad at their trunks that three men cannot reach around them. One can only imagine the original pine forests.

If the lumbermen had difficulty reaching them, the challenge is no easier for today's adventurer. Although they are preserved in a 650-acre park reserve about 40 kilometres west of Dorset, the only way to reach them are by canoe or by snowmobile. If by canoe, then the trees lie on the portage between Minkey and Dividing Lake, accessible from either Sword and Dagger lakes in Haliburton or from Smoke, Ragged and Big Porcupine lakes in Algonquin Park. If by snowmobile, the local snowmobile club at Dwight and Dorset has laid out a trail specifically to view the giant trees.

In 1984 Alan Pope, then Ontario's Minister of Natural Resources, declared the white pine to be Ontario's official provincial tree. Describing its "sweeping limbs and ragged foliage silhouetted against the sky," he lauded it as a "splendid arboreal symbol, a family tree." How bitterly ironic that the depletion of the white pine also symbolizes the victory of greed over natural heritage, the conquest of waste over conservation. More recently the Ontario government has approved controversial logging in the Temagami area, Ontario's last true pine wilderness.

As the giants of Haliburton age and die, as the largest of them are now doing, they will take with them the final vestiges of Ontario's primeval wilderness.

The last big pines.
- Ontario Ministry of Natural Resources

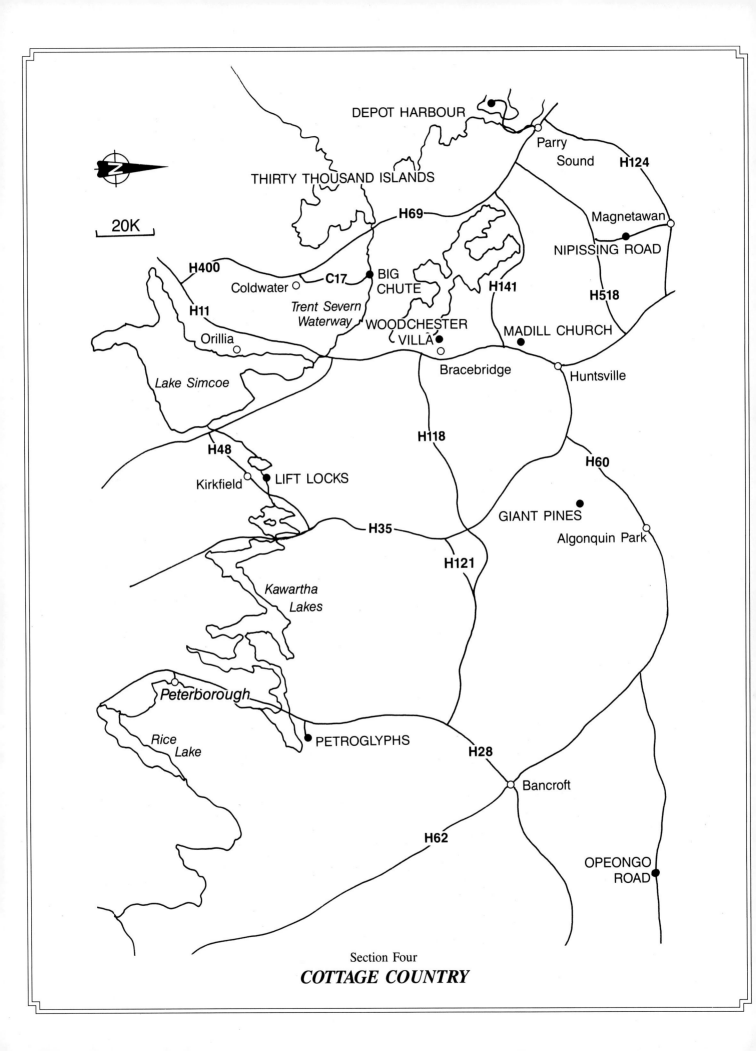

DEPOT HARBOUR

Parry
Sound **H124**

THIRTY THOUSAND ISLANDS

H69

Magnetawan

NIPISSING ROAD

20K

H400

Coldwater ○ **C17** BIG
CHUTE

H141

H518

H11

*Trent Severn
Waterway*

WOODCHESTER
VILLA

MADILL CHURCH

Orillia ○

Bracebridge

Huntsville

Lake Simcoe

H118

H60

H48

Kirkfield ○ ● LIFT LOCKS

GIANT PINES

H35

Algonquin Park ○

H121

*Kawartha
Lakes*

Peterborough

*Rice
Lake*

● PETROGLYPHS

H28

Bancroft

H62

OPEONGO
ROAD

Section Four
COTTAGE COUNTRY

28
The Opeongo: A Mountain Road

To satisfy intense lobbying by lumber companies, in 1855 the Canada West government of William Lyon MacKenzie embarked upon what it called the Great Colonization Road Scheme. Others would call it the Great Colonization Road Scam. Desperate for men, horses and food in their cutting camps, the lumber companies convinced MacKenzie's government to lure settlers into the rocky upland which lay between the Ottawa River and Georgian Bay with grand announcements of free land on rich soil. The land in reality was so rocky that it could scarcely hold the surveyors' stakes. And MacKenzie knew it.

The first of 25 free grant colonization roads, the Opeongo, twists its way through southern Renfrew County. With the collapse of the scheme it was one of the few to retain a population of farmers, most of whom yet work off the farm to supplement their meagre farm incomes.

As a result, much of the old road retains an extensive pioneer landscape unequaled elsewhere in Ontario. Here in the heart of the Black Donald Mountains the road winds past snake rail fences and cabins, many yet occupied by descendants of the original pioneers. Along it are a rare barn style known as "string barns," where pioneers too poor to replace their original structures merely added on

to them. As the road lurches up the mountainsides, it yields vast panoramas that stretch to the distant Gatineau Mountains in Quebec. So unusual is the entire landscape that a staff report by the Ministry of Natural Resources recommended the entire route be preserved as an historical park. Displaying its customary disdain for heritage preservation, that ministry ignored its own report.

But until it has been ruined by redevelopment, the Opeongo Road will continue to offer a glimpse of another era. Beginning at Dacre on Highway 132, a one-time stopover town with a weathered main street out of another day, the drive will lead you westward up the steep face of the Black Donald Mountains, where the Ottawa Valley drops away at your feet. It leads you past the dirt trail to the abandoned pioneer settlement of Newfoundout, through the now empty radar base at Foymount and to the ghost town of Brudenell, where an old store and hotel once played host to pioneer travellers and farmers.

Between Brudenell and Barry's Bay, the Opeongo has changed little. The road is narrow, unpaved and twists around hills of grey granite which are covered with forest and separated by gullies and small valleys. It is a landscape that yet contains the log barns and small fields once owned by hopeful pioneer settlers when dreams were still grand.

Log farms were once plentiful on the historic Opeongo Road.

29
The Nipissing Road of Broken Dreams

One of the last of the troubled roads was the Nipissing. Completed in 1875, it lurched and twisted over the rocky barrens from Rosseau (on the lake of the same name) to Nipissing.

As long as the lumber companies were busy, the roadside settlers prospered. Pioneer clearings dotted the forest between the growing stopover villages. But by the turn of the century the forest was cleared. When the lumber companies left, so too did the settlers' source of winter work and produce sales. The flight from the roads became a rout as disheartened settlers, some starving, left for the Canadian and American west. Forests claimed the tiny clearings and the once-bustling villages became sagging ghost towns.

Among the more than 20 failed colonization roads, the Nipissing has changed the least. The story of its hardship is reflected in cellar holes, decaying barns, empty cabins and ghost towns.

Two of the most interesting relics lie along its southern half between Highway 518 and Highway 124. Here lie the dozen buildings of the ghost town of Seguin Falls (near the intersection of the Nipissing and Highway 518), including workers' cabins, a large wooden mansion and the site of the King George Hotel. A few kilometres north, in the Dufferin Methodist cemetery, a tragic story is told. Here, a pair of tombstones recount the deaths of ten children, all under ten and all within a two-week period in 1902. Nothing on any other colonization road more graphically depicts the hardships faced by pioneer settlers.

The most rugged portion of the road lies north of Magnetawan between Highway 124 and Highway 522. Along it you will encounter the empty hotels of Mecunoma (otherwise known more colourfully as Bummers Roost) and the elaborately fretted wooden general store at Commanda, now a living museum.

While many of the old colonization roads have been paved to speed cottagers to the busy lakes of central Ontario, the Nipissing, more than any of the others, vividly depicts a time when dreams of hope became nightmares of hardship.

A tombstone on the Nipissing Road reflects the often tragic hardships endured by the colonization road pioneers

30
Madill Log Church

Nothing conjures visions of Ontario's pioneer heritage better than the log buildings built by the pioneers' own hands. Most lasted only a few years and were soon replaced by larger structures. A few however have endured.

One of the most solid survivors from this pioneer past is the Madill log church near provincial Highway 11, only seven kilometres south of the busy tourist town of Huntsville.

The temptation of free land offered under Ontario's ill-fated colonization road scheme lured Irishman John Madill to this tract of land on what was then the rugged Muskoka Road. From his parcel he donated one acre for a church and cemetery.

Instantly the other area pioneers, in need of a permanent place to worship, donated precious logs from their land or their own brawny backs as axemen. Within months, where there had been only bush and raw ground, a church, solid and solemn, its freshly cut pine logs cut square by the pioneer workmen, gleamed yellow in the Muskoka sun.

Along the old pioneer roads that twist and snake through the rocky upland of the Canadian Shield, several log churches have indeed survived. But no other has continued in use (the United Church of Canada holds a special service each summer) and no other had such loving attention paid to the simple but beautiful detail of its windows and its form. In its cemetery the graves of the Madill family stand as permanent testimony to the spirit of its original benefactors and of the Muskoka pioneers.

The Madill log church is one of Ontario's best surviving examples of a pioneer log church.

31

Boats on Rails: The Big Chute Marine Railway

The groaning lift locks at Peterborough and Kirkfield are not the only unusual structures on the Trent Severn Waterway. Forty kilometres north of Barrie, County Road 34 leaves the village of Coldwater and takes you 20 kilometres along a winding road, past farms and through forests, to the Big Chute Marine Railway.

By the turn of the century, urbanites fed up with the noise and fumes of the industrial cities were finding a tranquil escape at places like the mouth of the Severn River. By 1916 there was increasing pressure to open up still more of the Severn, and the federal government gave approval to a marine railway that would guide the boats over the steep falls known as the Big Chute. (A temporary railway already existed for workers then constructing a hydro generating station at the same location.)

In 1920 the marine railway was finished, but by 1922 it needed enlarging. The new car was 14 feet by 34 feet. It operated by being lowered into the water at one end, where the boats could be bloated over the carriage and secured. The carriage was then winched out of the water. When it reached the height of land, the cables were manually switched for the descent into the water at the other end. Following the Second World War, recreational boating experienced an unprecedented boom. By the 1970s the outdated marine railway had become such a bottleneck that considerable enlargement was necessary. In 1980 a new carriage, 40 feet by 80 feet, began to rumble up and down the granite cliff. Unlike the old car, the new carriage uses a modern system of four winches operated by digital control and automatic cable transfer. The older historic car is still used to handle overflow.

Viewing is easy. Parks Canada has created an attractive park with hiking and picnicking facilities. Amid the picnic benches, you may see concrete steps. These once led to the large houses that were home to original workers in the hydro electric plant.

But it's the sight of an 80-foot yacht creaking up a cliff on a railway car that you won't easily forget.

The older of the cable cars at the Big Chute Marine Railway now handles overflow traffic.

32
The Trent Canal Lift Locks

Snaking through the middle of Ontario is a natural water highway, a chain of lakes linked by short streams that connect Lake Ontario on the east and Georgian Bay on the west. Its name is familiar to most Ontarians as the Trent Severn Waterway. To Ontario's early settlers it was their life line, their only highway. Along its lakes, especially the Kawarthas, they floated out their logs, took their wheat to the mill, and travelled for their food.

Although the first pioneers cried for canals to link the lakes and rivers as early as the 1820s, governments dithered and did not act until 1892, when the Department of Railways and Canals took over the system and constructed the first major system of canals and locks.

But at Peterborough and Kirkfield, the flow of water fell so steeply that four costly and time-consuming locks would be required at each location. The engineers at Montreal's Dominion Bridge Company, contractor for the canal, looked to an insignificant village in England named Weaver Creek. There the locks on the canal were operated by an unusual system known as hydraulic lift locks. Two watertight boxes, each big enough to hold a vessel, were balanced hydraulically side by side. As the upper box filled, it became heavier than the lower box and descended,

forcing the lower box to the upper level. Savings over traditional locks, both in time and construction cost, were enormous.

In 1904 Ontario gazed in awe as two such lift locks groaned into operation at Peterborough and Kirkfield. The larger of the two, at Peterborough, was 65 feet and at the time the highest in the world (by comparison Kirkfield's is 50 feet). Indeed the only others were in England, Belgium and France. And today they remain the only two of their kind on this continent.

But they were too late to help the settlers. By then the countless little railway companies had created a dense network of railway lines that made water transportation obsolete, except for recreation.

Today that remains the sole function of the Trent Canal and its lift locks. To reflect this emphasis, the whole Trent Canal system is run by the federal department responsible for recreation, Parks Canada.

Even for landlubbers the sight of a bucket of boats high in the air has become a tourist attraction. The lock at Kirkfield is accessible by following signs from Highway 48 in that village, while that at Peterborough is found by following signs from Highway 28.

"There's a boat over your head".

The great lift locks at Peterborough and Kirkfield are the only pair of their kind in North America.

33
Eight Sides to a House

During the first two generations of Ontario's European settlement, house styles were fairly uniform. From log cabins to Georgian mansions, the pattern was consistently boxy. But with affluence and stability, and with the increasing artistic curiosity of the late Victorian age, there came more architectural experimentation. With it came one of the more unusual house styles ever seen in Ontario, and indeed in northeastern North America, the eight-sided house.

The origin of the design is credited to an amateur architect, American Orson Fowler, who featured it in his 1848 book *A Home for All*. Its advantages, he argued, were that a greater floor space to wall space ratio made it cheaper to build, and with more external wall space for windows, it was brighter and therefore healthier.

Henry Bird apparently agreed. In 1882 he built one of Ontario's first octagonal houses in what was then a raw frontier town named Bracebridge. "Woodchester Villa"

has remained remarkably well preserved and has been declared a heritage building by the town of Bracebridge. Located on King Street, it is open year-round (daily in the summer) to visitors.

The style had many imitators and by 1900 Ontario could boast more than 100 octagonal houses. Today fewer than half remain, most in central or eastern Ontario, including Lowville, Huttonville, Maple, Picton, Calabogie and Hawkesbury, the latter town also claiming an octagonal barn. Ontario's northernmost multi-sided building is the popular "round barn" near Sault Ste. Marie along the Trans-Canada Highway.

But the popularity of the octagonal houses suffered not from cost or aesthetics but from the more pragmatic problem of trying to arrange rectangular furniture in triangular rooms. And so it is unlikely that this interesting experiment will remain anything more than an unusual sidebar in Ontario's architectural history.

Woodchester Villa, Bracebridge.

34
Depot Harbour: A Ghost Town Worth Visiting

If you are a ghost-town enthusiast, the Parry Sound area offers one of Ontario's richest ghost-town grounds and one of its most rewarding ghost-town sites.

During its heyday Depot Harbour was a smoky railway terminus and Great Lakes port, and with its 3,000 residents it threatened to eclipse places like Midland and Owen Sound. But today the wind blows across cracked sidewalks and overgrown foundations as Georgian Bay's waves now lap against silent shores.

It all began nearly 100 years ago, when lumber baron John Rudolphus Booth forged a rail link across the middle of Ontario, from Ottawa to Georgian Bay and through Algonquin Park. His Ottawa, Arnprior & Parry Sound Railway would thereby not only access his rich pine limits in the park, but would also give Canada's western grain growers their most direct route to the ice-free Atlantic Ocean ports.

Booth's most serious obstacle came in an unlikely place, the proposed terminus of Parry Sound. Rebuffed by the high prices that Parry Sounders were demanding for their land, Booth built his own town. On Parry Island, beside the Great Lakes' largest natural harbour, Booth built Depot Harbour, a town of more than 100 dwellings, 3 churches, a school, railway yards and roundhouse, and 2 enormous grain elevators.

The place boomed for three decades and seemed destined to become one of the Great Lakes' busiest ports. Then, in 1928, the Canadian National Railways, which had assumed Booth's assets, relocated the railway facilities. Five years later a freak ice floe wrecked a trestle in Algonquin Park and severed Depot Harbour's life line. It never recovered. In 1945 the elevators, then storing cordite, erupted into a midnight fireball and Depot Harbour's story was over.

Before you even reach Parry Island you encounter one of Ontario's more unusual bridges, Booth's railway swing bridge, planked in to allow car traffic. Only now you need not watch for trains, for Booth's railway line has at last been lifted. Then at Depot Harbour itself you suddenly encounter the massive grey arches of the railway roundhouse looming from the underbrush like some ancient Roman ruin. Beyond it lie dozens of foundations and old sidewalks which comprise the most extensive of Ontario's 300 ghost towns. The best times to visit are early spring and late fall, when the absence of vegetation allows you to see and probe unimpeded one of Ontario's largest ghostly links with its past.

The grey arches of a one-time railway roundhouse peer from the woods at the site of the once bustling port of Depot Harbour.

35
Thirty Thousand Islands

T hey have been likened to the Greek islands of the Aegean Sea; they have provided Canada's famed Group of Seven artists with some of their most popular and enduring images; and they have lured more ships to a watery grave than many a war. They are Georgian Bay's Thirty Thousand Islands.

Even 30,000 is a modest underestimate, for when all the shoals, rocks and islands are added up, their number swells to more than 100,000. Their maze of back channels, their barren windswept headlands and their now familiar bent pines make these waters one of the most visually inspiring recreational experiences that North America can provide.

This seemingly endless archipelago begins at the long limestone peninsulas at Waubaushene, on the south end of Georgian Bay, and ends at the looming white knobs of the Lacloche Mountains at Killarney in the north.

This confusing and seemingly impenetrable maze, with its terrifying storms and countless hidden shoals, held permanent settlement at bay until the latter years of the 19th century. Only when southern Ontario's timber resources were gone and when railways finally reached Georgian Bay's southern shore did lumbering interests cautiously move up the bay. By 1880 the shoreline had been transformed. Lumber towns had sprung up in places like Muskoka Mills, Byng Inlet, French River and Collins Inlet. Summer fishing villages thrived on the larger island groupings such as the Minks and the Bustards, while Parry Sound and Depot Harbour became important lake ports.

Increased settlement brought increased tragedy. The mystery of the *Waubuno*, which went to its watery grave in a vicious November squall, has never been solved. Its cabin and engine were found several kilometres offshore, while its hull floated into the Moon River basin, where it can be easily seen and explored to this day.

Thanks to up-to-date detailed navigational charts and to improved channel markings, you can safely explore the Thirty Thousand Islands with your family. Although much of the shoreline south of the Moon River Basin is now choked with badly planned cottage development, the Moon River Basin itself has been preserved in a provincial park. North of Parry Sound many of the headlands and bays have remained free from the more intense development pressures. Here boaters can fish for pike, explore abandoned townsites and coal docks (all the once busy industrial towns save Parry Sound and Britt have become weedy ghost towns) or camp and watch the sunset with little more company than the crows and the gulls. As you survey the sculpted rock of the islands and shoals, and listen to the winds moaning in the grotesquely-shaped pines, you will lose any doubt that you are in a world-class scenic spot.

The Island Queen tourist vessel inches its way through the "Hole in the Wall," one of the myriad channels in the Thirty Thousand Islands maze.

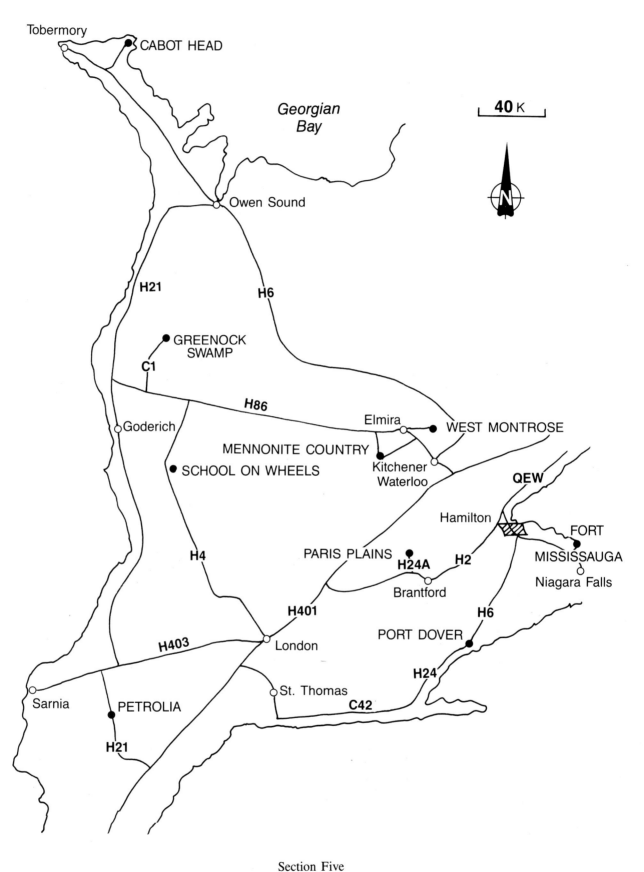

Tobermory

● CABOT HEAD

Georgian Bay

40 K

N

Owen Sound

H21

H6

● GREENOCK SWAMP

C1

H86

Goderich

Elmira

● WEST MONTROSE

MENNONITE COUNTRY

● SCHOOL ON WHEELS

Kitchener Waterloo

QEW

Hamilton

H4

PARIS PLAINS ● **H24A** **H2**

FORT MISSISSAUGA

Niagara Falls

Brantford

H6

H401

H403

London

PORT DOVER ●

Sarnia

● PETROLIA

St. Thomas

H24

C42

H21

Section Five
THE SOUTHWEST

36
Cabot Head: Remote Tranquility

In bustling southern Ontario any location that frees you from crowds and traffic ranks as unusual, especially if you can drive to it. Cabot Head, on the tip of the Bruce Peninsula, rates as one of the most idyllic of such getaways as southern Ontario can offer.

At the tip of the Bruce the rugged grey cliffs of the Niagara Escarpment plunge out of sight beneath the crashing waves of Lake Huron. Averaging 15 kilometres wide and 100 kilometres long, the Peninsula was a century ago the site of logging and pioneer farming. But once the logs were gone the farmers followed and the Peninsula became the destination of naturalists, cottagers and pleasure drivers.

The dead-end road to Cabot Head begins at Dyers Bay, just south of Tobermory and adjacent to Canada's newest national park, the Bruce Peninsula National Park. The road hugs the shoreline for about 12 kilometres until it ends at a rocky windswept headland known as Cabot Head. On one side forested limestone cliffs tower overhead, while on the other clear blue waters of Georgian Bay wash against a beach of white limestone boulders.

Halfway along, the road crosses a culvert and the ruins of an unusual lumbering operation. Here in 1880 Horace Lymburner constructed a steep flume from the rocky heights of the cliff, down which he flushed his logs to a pond beside his mill at the base, from which they were milled and shipped. You can yet explore the ruins of the flume and cribbing.

Cabot Head itself was once home to a sawmill and a small fishing fleet. But all that remains now is a lonely wooden lighthouse which once guided vessels around the perilous point of the peninsula. Here, where the only sounds are those of the wind and the gulls, you may be hard put to believe that urban Ontario is only hours away.

A seemingly endless boulder beach on the quiet road to Cabot Head on the Bruce Peninsula.

37
Petrolia Discovery

So vast, modern and international has today's petroleum industry become that its modest roots have been forgotten. And those roots go back to a handsome little town in southwestern Ontario aptly named Petrolia, where today a non-profit foundation named Petrolia Discovery is nobly striving to keep those roots alive.

And it is succeeding. On the perifery of the town, Petrolia Discovery operates a most unusual park. Here, on one of Canada's original oil fields, it operates oil rigs that date back a century. A central pumping plant, known in the industry as a Fitzgerald Rig, contains the biggest drive wheel ever built for a jerker rod system and has been operating off and on since 1903. From this building wooden jerker rods swing back and forth across the field to operate pumps which urge oil from the ground beneath ancient three-pole derricks.

You can also see the original gum beds that drew the first oil explorers to the area, and a cribbed well which shows how at first oil was dug rather than drilled.

The world's first commercial oil well began drawing oil from the ground 12 kilometres from Petrolia, at Oil Springs (this location is preserved on the grounds of the Oil Springs Museum). But it was at Petrolia that the larger fields were eventually found. By 1866 Petrolia had become a grimy boom town of 3,000 and was soon a terminus for branch lines from both the Grand Trunk and the Canada Southern railways.

The Petrolia Discovery theme park near the site of North America's first commercial oil well contains rigs and derricks that date back to the last century.

Then, with the formation of Imperial Oil Company in 1880, Petrolia became the centre of the world's oil industry. From Petrolia, drillers and riggers travelled to all corners of the world, sharing knowledge and skills that had quickly become legendary.

The years that followed the First World War were not kind to Petrolia. Multinational oil companies gobbled up the local companies, and the vast oil fields of the Turner Valley and later Leduc eclipsed Petrolia's more modest reserves. By the 1960s cracked sidewalks and vacant stores had turned Petrolia into a near ghost town.

But Petrolia Discovery has turned it around. By bringing to the present a living snapshot of the oil industry's past, the park has revived the entire town. The business community has pumped tens of thousands of their dollars into a brand-new streetscape which incorporates oil derrick designs into its lamp standards; the grand old opera house has been modernized, reorganized and reopened to travelling theatre companies; tours are conducted of the many mansions built by the world's earliest oil barons.

The park not only houses the old rigs, but also provides movies and photographs of the days when the eyes of the world focused on a small Ontario town that time had nearly forgotten.

(A Postscript: in January 1989 the residents of Petrolia awoke to find their cherished opera house gutted by fire.)

38
Return of the Fleet: Port Dover

A grey pre-dawn mist rolls around the looming cliff. The stubby white fishing boats glide across the calm waters and vanish into the fog. A scene from rocky Newfoundland or mountainous B.C.? Neither. It is the morning routine in the harbour of Lake Erie's Port Dover, home of the world's largest freshwater fishing fleet.

Canada's freshwater lakes have long remained a silent chapter in the story of Canada's fishing fleets. Yet commercial freshwater fishing is vital to the well-being of many of Canada's interior communities. Lake Winnipeg, Lake Athabaska, and Great Slave Lake all boast fishing fleets, as do northern Ontario's Lake of the Woods and Lake Nipigon, lakes that are more renowned for their recreational fishing.

But it is the Great Lakes that boast the largest freshwater fishing fleets, not just in Canada, but in the world. And the biggest of all calls its home Port Dover.

Port Dover, 70 kilometres southwest of Hamilton, began life as a Loyalist mill town. When during the 1812 War the Americans burned most of Lake Erie's mills, the townspeople looked to the lake for economic recovery. Soon the harbour bustled with schooners carrying lumber and barley, and small fishing boats. However it was not until the 1860s and 1870s, when the railways opened the American and European markets, that commercial fishing began in earnest. The enclosed diesel-operated "turtle back" fishing boats replaced the small one-man open skiffs and remain today the most common sight in a fishing port.

Pollution and predators, notably the sea lamprey, dealt commercial fishing a near mortal blow during the 1950s and 60s. But successful fish-stocking programs have restored at least partially the Great Lakes fishery.

By afternoon the sun has long burnt away the morning mist. On the horizon the round white forms grow larger. Soon a long string of fishing boats takes shape, churning a foamy wake before them and followed by a noisy throng of diving gulls. The tugs chug around the lighthouse and glide past the breakwater before turning toward their slips at the modern federal fishing marina. Nowhere else in Ontario can you so easily witness the return of so large a fleet. More than 40 in number, they pile their silvery catch of yellow perch and walleye into large crates filled with ice. While most are destined for fish counters in Toronto or the U.S., many end up in local stores.

In the evening you can head for the Erie Beach Hotel, a restaurant with a wide reputation for its dinners of fresh yellow perch. From your table you might watch the dusk turn the lake into pastel shades of blue, pink and orange while the fishermen rest up for another dawn.

The world's largest freshwater fishing fleet calls Port Dover its home.

39
Horse and Buggy Days

The doors of the simple white church swing open. Suddenly the steps fill with black-garbed women and children of the Old Order Mennonites, while from behind the church the black-hatted men urge their horse-drawn buggies. A crowd gathered across the road swings into action, cameras clicking and videos whirring as the horse-drawn procession clatters off down the dusty county road.

The scene is a typical Sunday morning around a Mennonite Meeting House in northern Waterloo Region, a rich, rolling farmland settled in 1786 by hundreds of Old Order Mennonites from Pennsylvania. The Mennonite movement began in the 16th century when Menno Simons led his German and Dutch followers from the mainstream Protestant religions into a pacifist doctrine. Incessant government persecution eventually forced them to the religious freedom of the U.S. and Canada. Their descendants, now in the thousands, still practise an orthodox agricultural lifestyle "deprived" of such comforts as electricity, indoor plumbing, cars and modern clothing.

Although they cling to a set of values far different from those that surround and encroach upon them, Mennonites are not isolationist. Indeed they participate willingly in their communities and are usually more amused than annoyed at the incessant stares and camera lenses that are directed their way.

Mennonite country lies immediately west of the communities of Elmira and St. Jacobs. Here the discreet observer can revisit scenes out of another era. Haying bees see several teams of horses drawing their cutters gracefully through the green fields of hay. During spring and fall, ploughing teams of up to eight or ten workhorses churn up great clouds of dust. But perhaps the truest scene from a bygone day is the Mennonite barn-raising. Hundreds of the black-garbed brethren can arrive in the pre-dawn to little more than the concrete foundation and sit down to the evening meal with the finished barn beside them. North America's largest buggy factory lies a few kilometres west of Elmira, while in St. Jacobs the "Meeting Place" is a museum dedicated to Mennonite history.

Some may shy away from "Mennonite watching," but there's no need. The Mennonites themselves proudly put forward their lifestyle. Their sense of community, their shunning of modern frills, and the more human scope and pace of their lives are a tonic and an example for today's frenzied urbanite.

Horses and buggies crowd the yard of a Mennonite meeting house.

Opposite:
A century-old tradition lives in this Mennonite barn-raising near Linwood, Ontario.

40
The Last Covered Bridge

The clatter of hoof beats and groaning of a wagon wheel echo among the wooden rafters of the old covered bridge. A scene from a western movie? No, an everyday event at West Montrose, Ontario, 15 kilometres north of Waterloo, just off Regional Road 22.

The area is heavily populated by the Old Order or "horse and buggy" Mennonites, and these black-garbed traditionalists frequently guide their horse-drawn wagons or buggies through what is Ontario's last covered bridge.

In an era when wood was cheap and commonly used for bridge construction, walls and roofs were often added to prevent the deterioration caused by rain and heavy snow. Despite their enormous popularity in Quebec and New Brunswick, where hundreds yet survive, covered bridges failed to catch on in Ontario. In fact only five were ever recorded. The covered bridge at West Montrose is the sole survivor.

It was completed in 1881 by John and Sam Bear. Until 1960 the 200-foot bridge with its 20 shuttered windows remained the only way to cross the Grand River for several miles around. Then a new concrete structure carried a new highway over the river just a short distance north. But rather than demolish the historic bridge, the municipal council of the Township of Woolich and Ontario's Department of Highways decided to preserve and mark it with an historic plaque. On August 28, 1960, the cloth drape was yanked off the plaque by one of the original workmen, John Geisel.

Not only has the bridge been saved, but unlike many of those preserved elsewhere it has been maintained in use, despite damaging ice floes, by using repair techniques sympathetic to its old style.

To complement this postcard scene, the village of West Montrose, huddled around the western approach to the bridge, has retained most of its simple 19th-century buildings.

A part of pioneer Ontario can be both seen and heard at the West Montrose covered bridge.

Of Ontario's five historic covered bridges, that at West Montrose on the Grand River is the only survivor.

41
Paris Plains Church

Ontario's cities and countryside contain many magnificent stone buildings, from the huge blocks of red sandstone that form the Queen's Park legislative buildings and the old city hall, both in Toronto, to the rubble stone that hardened pioneers gathered from their fields to make the handsome St. Margaret's church on the Bruce Peninsula.

But no stone construction is as rare or as delightful as the neat rows of cobblestones on the Paris Plains Church near the intersection of Provincial Highway 24A and Brant County Road 28 north of Paris, Ontario.

When Levi Boughton migrated from Rochester, New York, to Paris in the 1850s, he brought with him a construction technique that Upper Canadians had never before seen. Originally devised by the ancient Romans during their occupation of England, it was a technique that could utilize common fieldstones — the bane of many farmers in the Paris and Brantford areas — and create a building of rare beauty.

The technique involved gathering thousands of these stones, usually dolomite or limestone that had been relentlessly ground into spheres by the great glaciers and the swirling of their meltwaters. The stones would then be passed through a standard ring to ensure uniformity of shape and size. Then they would be laid in level "courses" to construct the walls of the buildings. The result was walls of incredibly straight rows of cobblestones, almost as if they had been handmade.

The contractor for the church, as for other buildings in Paris, was Philo Hull. And Paris, with more than a dozen surviving examples, remains the centre of this technique. Few other areas of Ontario had either the bounty of the otherwise cursed fieldstones or the skills in building with them. Later in the century, when brickmaking made construction so much cheaper, Boughton's cobblestone style died completely. Occasionally it is resurrected in individual homes, not because it is cheaper, but because of its rare beauty and grace. In Boughton's day it was an inventive way to turn a thing of nuisance into a thing of beauty.

The unusual cobblestone walls on the Paris Plains Church near Brantford.

42
Fort Mississauga: The Forgotten Fort

Neglected and forgotten Niagara-on-the-Lake's Fort Mississauga now endures a barrage of golf balls from the course on which it sits.

Round and hard, the missiles speed through the air, crashing against the walls of the ancient fort. Bricks and mortar splatter into the air and fall to the ground.

Niagara-on-the-Lake's Fort Mississauga is not being assaulted by enemy batteries but rather by errant golfers on the golf course that now surrounds it. Although the fort was hurriedly erected in 1814 to stave off a repeat of the earlier American devastation, Fort Mississauga never had a hostile missile shot at it — that is, not until the 20th century, when the grounds were leased by a golf course and golf balls smashed into it with regularity. As a structure, it is unimpressive. Even when manned, its garrison consisted of a corporal and three privates. One 19th-century writer was moved to liken it to a "dilapidated brewery."

In 1976, when Parks Canada — which had so masterfully restored the much larger Fort George a short distance away — indicated its intention to restore Fort Mississauga, the golfers rebelled. Although Parks Canada has retained ownership and has stabilized the walls, they have left the fort a ruin. And that is what makes the fort unusual. It sits in the middle of the golf course, otherwise untouched since its abandonment in 1870. Picturesque and silent, it gazes across the Niagara River, waiting for hostile missiles that now come flying at it from behind.

Fort Mississauga sits in the middle of the historic town of Niagara-on-the-Lake and is accessible by walking along the river bank from the corner of Front and Simcoe streets.

The town, of course, has much to offer the history lover, for it has remained largely untouched for more than a century. The restored Fort George is worth a visit, as is the Niagara Apothecary, reputedly Ontario's oldest drugstore and now run by the Ontario College of Pharmacy as a Confederation-era drugstore.

43
The Great Greenock Swamp

Grey and Bruce counties; here the dirt farm roads roll past sturdy houses of brick or stone, past solid barns and herds of grazing beef cattle. Far from the reach of the urban sprawl and country estates that are so quickly gobbling up what remains of Ontario's valuable prime farmland, the area is one of Ontario's last truly rural bastions.

But in the middle of prosperous Bruce County, many of the dusty roads come to a sudden halt at a dark wall of tall trees surrounded by stagnant water. One of southern Ontario's last stretches of untamed wilderness, it is the Great Greenock Swamp.

The swamp dates from the retreat of the last great glaciers that once covered all of southern Ontario to a depth of 2 - 3 kilometres. As waters from the melting ice poured southward then west, they were halted by a ridge of sand and gravel to form a huge pond. The pond never fully drained away and left the 10,000 ha water-logged forest that remains to this day.

After 1850 settlers poured into the wilds of what was then called the Queen's Bush. Confronted by the impenetrable tangle, the settlers were forced to make their way around it. To this day fewer than half a dozen roads have managed to penetrate the mosquito-infested wilds. Those that do plunge straight through, for there are no hills or rivers to alter their course. The roads run tunnel-like through a canopy of tree branches until a glow at the end announces a clearing and the resumption of farmland.

A clutch of wooden pioneer villages clings to the fringes, with names like Riverside and Greenock, where inhabitants still speak with a Scots-Irish brogue that has long vanished in much of rural Ontario.

Dark and foreboding, the Great Greenock Swamp is perhaps the best visual reminder of the intimidating forest barriers that once confronted the early settlers in this part of Canada.

Abandoned farm on the periphery of Greenock Swamp.

44
The Schoolhouse That Rode the Rails

Most of us recall, some even fondly, the little red (or yellow, or stone) schoolhouses. For decades these dotted the Ontario countryside and were the educational mainstay of rural Ontario. Few of us are aware, however, that through the wilds of northern Ontario, where only the railroads linked little settlements isolated by miles of bush, the schoolhouses were in railway cars.

Of the seven schoolcars that once plied the North, only two survive. That at Clinton has become a museum to this little-remembered phenomenon.

Between 1880 and 1914 three great transcontinental railways drove their steel through northern Ontario's forbidding bushland. These were followed by the Algoma Central and the Temiskaming & Northern Ontario railways (later the Ontario Northland). At railside there grew a string of little settlements. Some were mere section villages of a half-dozen shacks, others were sizable mill towns built for the cutting and shipping of lumber. Only a handful of divisional towns or industrial towns grew to be large enough to support their own schools.

By 1922 the population of these isolated outposts was substantial, yet they had few facilities, no luxuries, and no schools. J.B. McDougall, a North Bay school inspector and principal, pleaded with then Ontario premier G. Howard Ferguson to initiate a six-month experiment which would bring to the settlements a school on the back of a train.

Passenger cars were reconstructed to contain classrooms and accommodation for the teacher. In 1926 the first two cars departed their display areas at the Canadian National Exhibition en route to their destinations in northeastern Ontario. The ''experiment'' proved so successful that it was quickly made a permanent program, and by 1938 seven such cars were operating across northern Ontario between Quebec and Manitoba. For four days at a time the cars would rest at a siding in the larger settlements while children hiked or sledded for several miles for their precious education. Night school was provided for adults and the schoolcars became social gathering places for the area.

However, after the 1950s the North began to change. The mill villages folded, especially after the large pulp companies began to take over the smaller sawmilling licences. A major highway construction program drew industrial activity to the larger centres and most of the railside settlements became ghost towns. By the late 60s the schoolcars were no longer needed, and one of the last, C.N.R. #15089, was shunted unceremoniously into a Toronto railyard in 1967.

After spending a few years with the Ontario Rail Association, car 15089 was put up for sale. A former student noticed the ad and eagerly phoned the family of the car's last teacher, Fred Sloman. (Fred Sloman was also the teacher who participated in the program the longest, from its inception in 1926 up to his retirement in 1965.) To the credit of the community, the people of Clinton, the home of Fred Sloman's widow, Cela, rallied behind the cause and brought the car to Clinton, where it was restored to its original state and opened as a museum.

It's worth a look. For while recycled schoolhouses are commonplace, the schoolhouse that rode on rails is one of a kind and retells a story of northern life that would otherwise be forgotten.

The School On Wheels, Clinton, Ontario.

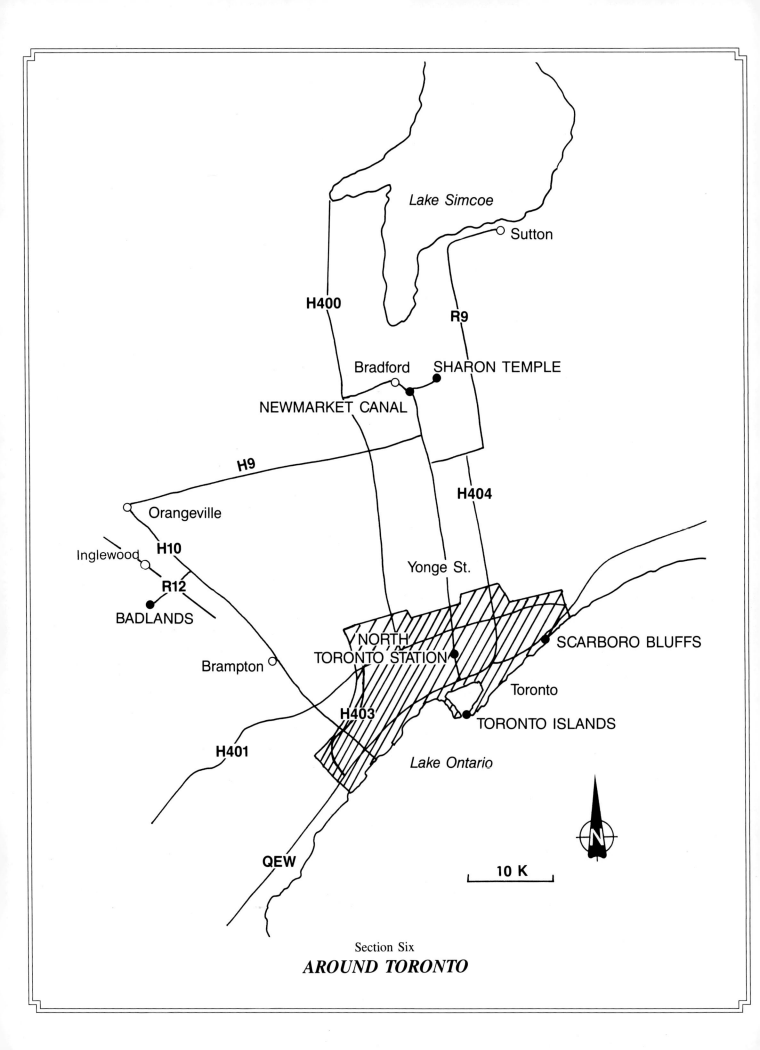

Lake Simcoe

○ Sutton

H400

R9

Bradford

SHARON TEMPLE

NEWMARKET CANAL

H9

H404

○ Orangeville

Yonge St.

Inglewood

H10

R12

SCARBORO BLUFFS

BADLANDS

NORTH
TORONTO STATION

Brampton ○

Toronto

H403

TORONTO ISLANDS

H401

Lake Ontario

QEW

N

10 K

Section Six
AROUND TORONTO

45
Ontario's Badlands

Many westward-bound Ontarians make Drumheller, Alberta, one of their "must sees." For here thousands of years of water and wind erosion have worn through layers of shale to create a landscape of barren hills and gullies punctuated by remnant pillars known as "hoodoos." While the desert-like terrain spurned farmers and ranchers, it did expose coal seams, which spawned a string of mining towns. Although most of the coal towns are now ghost towns, the shale did reveal another feature that has restored some vitality to the area: dinosaur bones. So plentiful and so well preserved are these fossils of giants long gone that they have sparked a tourist boom.

What makes Ontario's badlands so unusual is that they are totally unexpected, a painted desert surrounded by fields and forests of green. Located in two areas, west of Inglewood and north of Aldershot, these barren knobs and gullies, like those at Drumheller, reveal colourful layers of green and red shale. The absence of a firmer caprock has prevented the formation of pillars, or hoodoos. Nor do the layers yield any fossils; they are too recent for that. While the shale dates from an ancient seabed, the badlands topography is man-made. For it was after the early settlers had cleared away the forests that the rains began to wash away the topsoil and carve into the soft shale.

Like those in Alberta, Ontario's badlands revealed an economic resource, the ingredients for brickmaking, that brought a boom to the Inglewood area and then left a legacy of diminished villages and ghost towns. Terra Cotta, now a quiet residential community, was originally a lusty town that boomed on the back of its brickmaking factories. Today only a handful of boom-time buildings stand amidst more modern luxury homes. Nearby, about two kilometres west of Cheltenham, a large brickyard created its own town. Here the gaunt shells of the now silent factory still stand like sentinels in an overgrown field. Their ultimate fate rests on the outcome of a battle between heritage conservationists who would preserve them and industrialists who would demolish them to extract more shale.

While the badlands themselves have yet to attract a rush of tourists, they have long been the destination of geology students and more recently of ghost-town tours conducted by the author.

An unexpected sight on Ontario's otherwise green landscape are these badlands near Cheltenham.

46
Ghost Canal

The wall of stone blocks looks enough like a canal lock, but eight metres below your feet, where water and boats should be, you see grass and trees. You are standing beside the remains of a canal that never saw water, the Newmarket Canal.

The early decades of the 19th century were the canal era. At a time when railways were little more than science fiction and roads little better than quagmires, water was the only highway. The remarkable success of the Erie Canal in New York state sparked a spate of canal-building in Ontario. The Welland, the Rideau, the Grand, as well as canalization of parts of the St. Lawrence and Trent, all made their appearance by 1840. And as early as 1800 surveyor General Smith produced a map showing a canal linking Lake Ontario with Lake Simcoe along the Rouge and Holland river systems.

But by the time the smoke of steam engines ushered in the railway era, around 1850, the Newmarket Canal still existed only on paper. With canals in decline, there seemed little point in proceeding. Then, in 1904, the Trent Canal was completed and politicians from the Newmarket area pushed once more for a link to that system. In 1905

Newmarket Canal, lock #2, Holland Landing.

they sent a delegation to Ottawa, and in 1906, much to their surprise, the federal government agreed. In 1907 construction began.

The canal was to be built in three sections. The first, from Lake Simcoe to Holland Landing, a distance of 15 kilometres, would be level and require no lock structures. The second, from Holland Landing to Newmarket, a distance of seven kilometres, would require three locks to cover the 14-metre rise in elevation. The third section would carry the canal to its completion at Aurora.

After the first two sections were finished, World War I intervened, and in 1916 the canal project was cancelled. No water ever passed through its three locks. One lock structure, minus gates, still stands in Holland Landing where old Yonge Street enters the village. Another, the best one to visit, lies about three kilometres east of Holland Landing. Here you can explore the old lock in the middle of the woods, while above the lock the local conservation authority maintains a park beside a small pond.

Although many Ontario canal projects either failed outright or declined economically, the Newmarket Canal remains as it began, high and dry.

This Holland Landing lock on the Newmarket Canal never saw water.

47
Temple of Light

Much like modern-day fundamentalism, the religious denominations of early Ontario were often fueled by the quirks and charisma of dominating leaders. Groups like the Quakers and the Shakers, the Mormons and the Mennonites, all originated with "visionaries" who led a group of dedicated followers away from the mainstream denominations. While all were present in pioneer Ontario, none left so prominent a landmark as did David Willson and his Children of Peace.

In 1801 David Willson, a Quaker, migrated from New York state to the Newmarket area of Upper Canada, where his Society of Friends brethren (as the Quakers were called) were particularly active. However Willson grew impatient with the local leadership and decided to have a vision of his own. His vision was to restore his form of Christianity to its Judaic roots. In contrast with the austere Quakers, an elaborate temple and vigorous music provided a focus for this type of religious worship.

In 1825 Willson and his Children of Peace began construction of an elaborate and highly symbolic temple. When finished, the three-storey structure resembled a windowed wedding cake and totally dominated the landscape of simple pioneer buildings. Centre doors on each side symbolized the equal acceptance of people from all directions, while the square shape, it is said, meant the group dealt "squarely" with everyone. Inside, the 12 pillars represented the 12 apostles.

Then as now, religious leaders displayed a strong sense of self. Inside the temple Willson placed an elaborate altar which was partially enclosed, while on the grounds outside the temple he built his small but equally elaborate personal study. The Children of Peace celebrated two festivals, Willson's own birthday, dubbed the "Feast of the Passover," and the fall "Feast of Illumination," when the Children placed 116 candles in their temple windows. Although frequently described as a religious imposter, Willson was acclaimed throughout Ontario for his lively travelling temple band.

Willson's death in 1866 signalled the downfall of the Children of Peace. By 1890 they were extinct and the temple vacant. But in 1919 a far-sighted York Pioneer and Historical Society (ahead of even some modern groups) acquired the temple and converted it into a museum.

And so it remains today. On the outskirts of Sharon, now a Toronto suburb, visitors may view the temple, little changed in a century and a half. Although pioneer implements now clutter the interior and other buildings have been located on the grounds, the story of Willson and his Children of Peace is well represented and brings to life a small but highly unusual chapter of our pioneer past.

"Sharon Temple"

One of the most unusual churches ever built in Ontario is this temple built by the equally unusual Quaker sect known as the Children of Peace.

48
The Dutch Chapel

One of southern Ontario's more unusual natural features is the Scarborough Bluffs. Not only does this craggy 20-kilometre-long form loom 100 metres over Lake Ontario, but its fractured and ever-eroding face reveals to scientists and laymen alike the mysteries of central Ontario's prehistoric past.

Unlike the tiny trickle that is today's Don River, Toronto was once the site of a mighty pre-glacial torrent greater than the St. Lawrence. Here, more than 70,000 years ago, these rushing waters poured into a great lake and there deposited an extensive delta. Then the Ice Age, with glaciers often more than two kilometres thick, deposited more boulder clay on top of the delta.

As the last ice sheets melted away 12,000 years ago and the lakes behind them drained, the delta stood like a mighty mesa above a barren landscape. Wind, water and frost then began to eat away at its southern face. The alternating layers of soft pure sand and rock-hard clay created odd-shaped pinnacles and buttresses. So closely did the rugged shoreline resemble his beloved English homeland, that Upper Canada's first governor, John Graves Simcoe, named them the Scarborough Bluffs.

In a quiet gully at the foot of Scarborough's Midland Avenue, erosion has created a series of buttresses, somewhat like the architecture found in medieval European chapels, and geologists have named the area the Dutch Chapel.

Most visit "the Bluffs," as they are called locally, to picnic in the landfill parks created by Metro Toronto at the foot of the cliffs. Some try to conquer the challenging trails that wind up their face. All, however, marvel at the towering heights. And as they look within the face of these cliffs, they can see a story that is 70,000 years old.

The Dutch Chapel, Scarborough Bluffs.

49
Toronto Islands' Haunted House

Ontario's oldest standing lighthouse is haunted, some say, by the ghost of its first keeper.

Constructed of huge limestone blocks, the 20-metre structure was built at Gibraltar Point, on what is now the Toronto Islands archipelago, in 1809, before there was a Toronto, before there were even islands. (In 1834 the Town of York became the City of Toronto. The islands were actually a peninsula until 1858, when a vicious storm hurled waves across its narrow sandy neck, severing it from the mainland.)

When the lighthouse was completed, John Paul Radelmuller was appointed its keeper and moved into a small log cabin beside it. In April 1813 he watched helplessly as American Colonel Cromwell Pearce guided 14 American ships past the lighthouse and landed troops that would capture York in one of the few American victories of the 1812 War.

Then, just two years later, Radelmuller disappeared. Although two men came to trial for his murder, the absence of a body led to their acquittal. Was he murdered by drunken companions? Did he renege on a bootlegging operation then being run from the military base? Despite recent research by self-proclaimed ''ghostbusters'' suggesting the latter, the answer will remain a mystery.

And it is a mystery anyone can explore. The lighthouse still stands on the Toronto Islands at Gibraltar Point, as it has for nearly two centuries. Although the former whale-oil lamp has long since been replaced by more modern navigational aids, the lighthouse remains virtually unaltered. Around it, an entire chapter in Toronto's history has started and finished. For several decades the islands were a popular recreational complex of amusement parks, hotels and private cottages. Today Gibraltar Point is a passive recreational area where trees, grass and trails have replaced the buildings of a bygone day. And the changes are all carefully watched over by the lighthouse and its keeper.

The old stone lighthouse on Toronto Islands' Gibraltar Point is said to be haunted by its first keeper.

50
North Toronto C.P.R.: The Station That Wasn't

The three decades that began in 1890 witnessed the construction of some of Canada's greatest railway stations: Montreal's Windsor Station, Ottawa's Union Station, Quebec's Gare du Palais, as well as large, columned stations in Vancouver, Winnipeg, Hamilton and Toronto. While Toronto's new Union Station, considered one of North America's best, was still on the drawing boards, there opened in the north end of the city, with great crowds and fanfare, what was Toronto's finest station to that time.

During the pre-World War I years the C.P.R. was rapidly expanding and enjoying great profits. However, it was being challenged by the upstart Canadian Northern Railway and the newly contructed Grand Trunk Pacific. To ensure its competitive edge and its corporate distinctiveness the C.P.R. decided to avoid the old Union Station on the waterfront and build its own grand station on its through line across what were then Toronto's northern limits.

It hired the Toronto architectural firm of Darling and Pearson to replace a small frame structure that had stood on the opposite side of Yonge Street. In 1916 their

work was unveiled for all to see. The crowds that jammed the waiting room and lined the platform were not disappointed. They gazed skyward at a 50-metre clock tower and marvelled at the brown-and-green marble walls that soared 10 metres in the waiting room and which brought light through three arching windows.

But what happened shocked the C.P.R., a company not used to failure. For after the crowds departed that day, they did not return. The huge new Union Station, which opened in 1923 near the site of the former station at the waterfront, could accommodate greater crowds and offered more trains to more places. C.P.R.'s grand station was a failure, and in 1930 it closed. Henceforth C.P.'s trains would also use Union Station. Eventually the cut-stone building was taken over by a liquor store, which covered over the decorative ceilings and the marble walls. But from the outside the building is little changed. Even though C.P.'s freight trains still rumble by, the line hasn't seen a passenger train for five decades. Happily, the building will be restored as part of Marathon Realty's plan to redevelop the area around it.

Despite its grand style and grander aspirations C.P.R.'s North Toronto station saw few passengers. It is now a liquor store.

photo by W.R.A. Brown

In his relentless quest for the unusual and the offbeat, writer, photographer and latter-day explorer Ron Brown has probed nearly every nook and back road in Ontario. In his many publications on ghost towns and back-road attractions, and in his frequent radio guest spots, he has shared his discoveries. His university background in geography and planning brought out the explorer early and he has spent much of the last quarter century on dusty roads and forest trails. And he is far from finished. There are many bends in the road that beckon yet.

Dear Reader,

We hope you've enjoyed this book. We hope you've enjoyed it enough to tell us some of the strange and wonderful things you've seen in your travels around Ontario. Please write to us at the address below. If we use your idea in *More Unusual Things* we'll give you credit and send a free book. Thanks.

> *More Unusual*
> c/o The Boston Mills Press
> 132 Main Street
> Erin, Ontario
> N0B 1T0